VICTORIOUS WORSHIP

*Winning in Life Through the Power of
Worthy, Wired, and Wise Worship*

Pastor Andre Mitchell

Renown Publishing
www.renownpublishing.com

Victorious Worship / Andre Mitchell
ISBN-13: 978-1-952602-80-1

To my wife, Devon, and my three children, Dreylen, Dylan, and Alonna. You guys are my peace and my motivation.

To the entire congregation of Deliverance Temple. This writing would not have been possible without your support, and I am so blessed and honored to be called your Pastor.

Lastly, this book is especially dedicated to my father, Bishop H. Royce Mitchell, who turned the pastorship of Deliverance Temple over to me in 2011 and who went home to glory on 10/05/2021. I pray this book touches hearts the way you have touched my life and others around the globe. I love you, Daddy.

CONTENTS

Foreword by
Dr. Terrance A. Bridges

As I reflect on the content of this text, I see more than pages of a book or curation of a sermonic script. I see the treasure of a man's life conceptualized in the written words. I consider the life and story of this author and what I have watched of his experience with my own eyes. I have seen in him a resilience in the face of resistance, fortitude in the midst of adversity, and a strength in the midst of loss. I believe that he lays out, in the text of this book, principles that have helped him to embody these values.

In my experience, I have come to know strength through worship. I have been on mountain tops of experience with God but also in valleys of sadness, loss, and feelings of defeat. It is worship that helped me to refocus on the most important thing. It is worship that renewed my sense of focus. It is worship that gave me hope and direction. With a magnifying glass, what we look at is able to grow in our sight and in our focus. Worship does the same regarding our awareness of the character and nature of Almighty God. Worship magnifies our focus of His divine attributes and minimizes the magnitude and view of our problems and frustrations. I believe this book authored by Pastor Mitchell helps to remind us of this fact and draw our attention back to what matters the most: worship of our creator.

Worship not simply with our lips, but worship that has been expressed through our lifestyle seems to be key. While there are many debates on how to worship among believers, traditions, and denominations, there is one thing that is clear: the "who" of our worship, and our focus upon the creator. This focus unlocks our potential as the creation. The person who can best navigate and maximize the features of a device is most likely to be the creator of that device. When there is a problem with the device, it is always best rectified by the manufacturer of the device. This is also true in the life of the believer. The maximum potential of the created is realized and unlocked by recognition and reference back to the creator. The correction of flaws and malfunctions is best resolved by reflection and redirection back to the creator. The admonishment of this author has done just that, directing our focus as the created back to our creator. Understanding and maximizing our giftings and purpose occurs as we reflect on and redirect our life actions based on the admonishments and principles found in this book.

As people, most of us do not invite pain as something desirable. In some sadistic cases, controlled pain is welcomed or tolerated, but uncontrollable and unplanned pain is not something that we welcome into our lives. Yet, pain has purpose, and pain has the potential to propel us forward in our walk with Christ if that pain is filtered through worship. Pastor Mitchell reminds me of the need to place pain properly through our worship and devotion to the creator. This book calls for the rededication of our thoughts, activities, and ideas back to the center of our life, God. Pastor Mitchell's words in these pages have fueled me toward continually seeking God's face and directing my affections toward Him—understanding that my pain doesn't have to be my ending but can propel me toward a fresh, new beginning in walking out the purpose and plan of Christ for my life through a life of worship.

I particularly remember this man of God being with me in one of the most difficult and painful moments of my life. As I sat on the front row of a church with a blueish-silver casket placed before me and the cold corpse of my ten-year-old laying in front of me, I was broken. I was in pain physically, emotionally, and spiritually. I could not understand or see the purpose of God in allowing the life of my son to slip through our fingers, or for him to move into eternity at such a young age.

But it was in this moment that the soothing presence of Christ in worship became real to me. It was not a song that was sung. It was not a word that was spoken or preached. It was not a kind gesture that was extended to bring relief. Although I appreciated it greatly, it was not the presence of people that provided the ultimate comfort. It was worship. And right there worshiping with me through the painful process of loss, the devastation of my situation, and the incomprehensible pain, was a brother and friend, Andre Mitchell. It was the power of worship that helped to heal my heart from this unbearable pain. It helped to redirect and refocus my attention on the character and centrality of God in my life's situation.

I felt much like David in the loss of his infant son:

David therefore sought God on behalf of the child. And David fasted and went in and lay all night on the ground. And the elders of his house stood beside him, to raise him from the ground, but he would not, nor did he eat food with them. On the seventh day the child died. And the servants of David were afraid to tell him that the child was dead, for they said, "Behold, while the child was yet alive, we spoke to him, and he did not listen to us. How then can we say to him the child is dead? He may do himself some harm." But when David saw that his servants were whispering together, David understood that the child was dead. And David said to his servants, "Is the child dead?" They said, "He is dead." Then David arose from the earth and washed and anointed himself and changed his clothes. And he went into the house of the Lord and worshiped. He then went to his own house. And when he asked, they set food before him, and he ate. Then his servants said to him, "What is this thing that you have done? You fasted and wept for the child while he was alive; but when the child died, you arose and ate food." He said, "While the child was still alive, I fasted and wept, for I said, 'Who knows whether the Lord will be gracious to me, that the child may live?' But now he is dead. Why should I fast? Can I bring him back again? I shall go to him, but he will not return to me."

—2 Samuel 12:16–23 (ESV)

I remember praying to God to resurrect my son. After all, I had prayed for deaf people and saw them receive their hearing. I had prayed for crippled people and watched them walk. I had prayed and cast out demons from young children whose families were entangled in Voodoo and Olbia. Surely, the Lord could raise my son's lifeless body off of the floor. Surely, the God who did these things for others could do it for me. I wept as I ran out of the house and knelt on the front lawn, crying out to God to raise my baby boy from the dead.

It didn't happen. He died. The emergency workers and coroner who were now on the scene just shook their heads in helplessness. That moment could have been the death of my faith, but instead, we began playing some of MarJ's favorite songs and worshiping. Tears streaming down from our eyes, and a mixture of moisture uncontrollably flowing from ours mouths and noses, we worshiped. Painfully and reluctantly, we worshiped. In this moment, like King David, I had to redirect my focus beyond earthly realities to the promises of eternity. Worship was what created this focus.

Again, as I sat in front of my son's lifeless body at the funeral, less than twenty feet away from me was Andre Mitchell, who joined me in worship. It was the collective worship that gave us hope in hopelessness. Life-filled hope in the midst of physical death. Joy through the heaviness of sorrow. I didn't understand or have the time to extrapolate the theological principles behind worship. I didn't have time to explain or articulate the level of cognitive dissonance and conflicting emotions. All I could do to survive was worship.

I am sure that this book will provide clarification and

explanation of some of those principles of worship and will lead believers to embrace the power of worship while sharpening their understanding of its truths. I know that as you peruse these pages, you will catch the inspiration to approach worship again with renewed fervor and faith. Andre Mitchell is a man who does not pontificate but who practices the truth behind the power of worship.

Maybe you are in pain and have a sense of hopelessness. It is my prayer that Pastor Mitchell's book renews your hope and strengthens your faith. While pain and pressure may remain, the power of worship can revolutionize your ability to successfully navigate their tough terrain. Let's read together, let's reflect on what is said through this work, but most of all, *let us leap* from the revelation in these pages to the place of worship!

The Power of Worship

Sometimes when we pray, we pray with mountain-moving faith, calling down power from on high into a situation. But how do we pray when we're in the valley, unsure if we'll survive another day? How do we pray if we don't know that we'll win?

Deep down, you know that you should have the faith to believe that you'll make it, but the truth is that you don't. You know that God loves you, but you sure don't feel Him right now. You know that Jesus has paid the price for your sins, but yielding to temptation seems like a much better idea than fighting yet another losing battle.

What's the use? You're saved, but you can't remember the last time you saw considerable growth in your spiritual life. Church is cool and all, but once it's over, you find yourself staring the same old problems in the face. The biggest problem of all stares back at you every time you look in the mirror. What can you possibly do in a predicament like this?

I have a one-word answer for you: worship. Yes, worship. Allow me to explain. One of the key elements of worship was revealed to us by the Master Himself. In John 4:23–24, Jesus said, "But the hour is coming, and is now here, when the true worshipers will worship the Father in spirit and truth, for the Father is seeking such people to worship him. God is spirit, and those who worship him must worship in spirit and truth."

WORSHIP REQUIRES HONESTY

You see, worship isn't just about being spiritual. It's also about being truthful. In moments of extreme pressure and affliction, it's important for us to be honest with ourselves and with God. Sometimes our troubles never get any better because we've trained ourselves to pretend that they don't exist. This is not God's idea of worship.

God is looking for people who, despite their problems, are still determined to find a way to give Him praise and adoration. Whether they cry, shout, sing, dance, lay prostrate, or sit in silence, they have decided that no matter what, God will get the glory in their circumstances. Now that's worship.

You don't have to figure out why these troubles have befallen you in order to worship. The pressure doesn't have to let up for you to worship. You don't have to see a clear solution for you to worship. You don't have to feel goosebumps or experience a smoke-filled room in order for you to worship. You can simply be truthful about what you are facing and call out to God like the psalmist did in Psalm 86:6–7:

"Give ear, O Lord, to my prayer; listen to my plea for grace. In the day of my trouble I call upon you, for you answer me."

No one experienced calamity and tragedy quite like Job did, yet this is how Scripture records his initial response to the loss of his children and his property:

> *Then Job arose and tore his robe and shaved his head and fell on the ground and worshiped. And he said, "Naked I came from my mother's womb, and naked shall I return. The Lord gave, and the Lord has taken away; blessed be the name of the Lord." In all this Job did not sin or charge God with wrong.*
> —*Job 1:20–22*

We need to worship regardless of our circumstances. In doing so, we're letting both heaven and earth know that when our hearts are overwhelmed, we can look to a God who is never stressed out, because He is higher than we are (Psalm 61:2 kjv). When we are broken, we can cry out to a God who remains whole. When we are sick, we know that we serve a God who is still a divine healer. When we are unrighteous, we can have confidence in a God who perfectly embodies righteousness and has bestowed His righteousness upon us.

This, to me, is authentic worship because in the midst of our trials, we reach an honest realization that we are nothing without God. We learn to trust Him. In the process of trusting Him, we come to know intimately that He can deliver us. It may take ten seconds, ten minutes, ten years, or maybe we won't receive it until eternity, but we know that He alone is capable of bringing us out of any circumstance. This posture transitions us from trial to victory because ultimately the victory is not in the result; the victory is in our decision to worship.

The first time Satan realizes that even your most confounding problems drive you to seek God, he will recognize that you're a lost cause. He knows that he will never have power or ascendency over you, because in good times or bad, you still have a heart that will worship. That's what it means to win. A Christian with the heart of a worshiper is a dangerous threat to the kingdom of darkness.

PURSUE A LIFESTYLE OF WORSHIP

I encourage you to ask God to allow a heart of worship to be birthed in you today. Then, as that heart continues to grow and mature in you, you will be able, like Paul, to declare boldly, "But thanks be to God, who in Christ always leads us in triumphal procession, and through us spreads the fragrance of the knowledge of him everywhere" (2 Corinthians 2:14). The power of worship is understanding that a heart cultivated for worship leads to a life connected to Christian victory.

To grow in a heart of worship, we must pursue a lifestyle of worship, and that requires developing a better understanding of what worship is and how to go about it in the right way. Over the course of this book, we will discuss how worship must be worthy, how worship must be wise and not wicked, and how worship must come from our new, God-given wiring rather than our faulty, fleshly wiring. We will conclude with three steps that will help you to win in the Lord as you worship Him in all circumstances. As we dig deeper into how to worship Him properly, we will discover just how worthy and faithful He is, and we will be reminded of His work in our lives.

I am eager to lead us in this exposition on worship. However, before we continue, I'd like us to begin our study from the launching pad of praise. It's commanded that if we are breathing, we should be praising: "Let everything that has breath praise the Lord!" (Psalm 150:6). Scripture encourages us to "enter his gates with thanksgiving, and his courts with praise!" (Psalm 100:4). Right where we are, before we move any further, let's start this journey by giving God glory and thanking Him for what He has already done.

CHAPTER ONE

Worthy Worship

I've always been fond of Psalm 29:1–2: "Ascribe to the LORD, O heavenly beings, ascribe to the LORD glory and strength. Ascribe to the LORD the glory due his name; worship the LORD in the splendor of holiness." Part of what I find so intriguing about this scripture is the instruction to "ascribe to the LORD the glory due his name," because it indicates that we can give glory to God in a way that is not due His name.

In other words, you can praise and worship God yet still fall short of understanding and acknowledging who He really is. We are to ascribe to Him the glory that is due His name, but we won't truly know His name until we know Him. The more we know Him, the more readily we grow in our ability to honor Him for who He is and what His name represents.

Our worship must be worthy of the God we claim to serve. It must have the proper value. The word *worship* comes from the Old English word *weorthscipe*, which pertained to acknowledging the worth of something.[1] It has the connotation of an appraisal, like that of a house you are planning to buy. If the house you're interested in is appraised at $250,000 and you offer $25,000, your offer will be laughed at and rejected because it's nowhere near what the house is worth.

If worship could be converted into money, our God is worth trillions upon trillions of dollars. Why is it that we can't—or won't—offer Him what He deserves?

WORSHIP IS A LIFESTYLE

In the old days, I viewed worship as equating only to styles of songs sung in a church service. I thought that worship was a slower song while praise was a faster song. That was the extent of my understanding of worship, but worship is not merely a slow song. It's deeper and more extensive than that. Ultimately, it's a daily lifestyle that proclaims, "God, I worship You because of who You are." That doesn't mean that every step you take will be perfect or that every decision you make will be the right one, but that your life as a whole worships God.

That's why we get up when we fall down. God is too worthy for us to stay down and give up. Since He paid the price for our sins, we can't stay in our sins. We have to change our mindset and move forward. Our lives must worship Him because He is worthy.

When you look back over your life, can you remember a time when God was not worthy? No! Now, there might have been times when you didn't know where He was, but even when you couldn't find Him, He was still worthy because He was still God. We cannot worship God based on what is currently happening in our lives. We have to worship Him based on His worth. That is how we win in life, by focusing on our God more than our problems.

When things are bad, God is still worthy of worship. When things are good, He is still worthy of worship. And when things are indifferent, He is still worthy of worship. Good, bad, indifferent, even ugly, He is still worthy, and we must give Him worthy worship.

What do we mean by worthy? *Worthy* means "having or showing the qualities or abilities that merit recognition in a specified way."[2] It also means to be deserving of effort, attention, or respect.[3] God is deserving of your effort, your attention, and your respect. Even when you're struggling with poor health, He is deserving of your effort. Sometimes you have to push past your tiredness, your anxiety, and your depression because He is still worthy. You have to push yourself to get to church. You have to push yourself to engage with God, push yourself to read the Bible and to spend time in prayer. You have to press into the things of God because He is always worthy, even when things aren't feeling right.

Now, what do we mean by worship? Worship is "reverence offered to a divine being or supernatural power" as well as the "act of expressing such reverence."[4] It can also be defined as "a form of religious practice with its creed and ritual,"[5] which is a definition that I want to encourage you to shift away from. That definition suggests that worship is a

9

routine, that it's just something we do, and that we may not even understand why we do it because it's simply a "religious practice."

I want to shift us away from religious practice and into relationship. Imagine that I have a specific routine that guides how I interact with my wife when I get home from work each day and that I have done this same thing every day for twenty-two years of marriage. When I walk through the door, I punch her lightly in the arm and say, "How's your day been?" In real life, my wife would not appreciate being greeted like a male friend, but for the purposes of this example, let's assume that this is my routine.

Say that when I come home from work one day, my wife is lying on the floor. When I ask her what's wrong, she tells me that she thinks she's suffering a stroke. Then, with no regard to the information she just gave, I punch her lightly in the arm and ask, "How's your day been?" That wouldn't make any sense, would it?

I would be operating out of a routine instead of operating out of relationship. If I'm operating out of relationship, I'd quickly shift into emergency mode. I would fully engage with the situation and figure out what's going on and what needs to be done. I'd try to get my wife immediate expert medical care. The point is that I wouldn't follow a routine, because my relationship would supersede my routine.

When it comes to God, however, some of us do things out of routine because we don't have a relationship with Him. We say our prayers every night before bed and recite the "Our Father" prayer. There's nothing wrong with having a set time to pray or praying the prayer that Jesus taught us in Scripture, but we need to make sure that we are worshiping God out of relationship rather than routine.

Our relationship with God should be what guides our lives. When we wake up in the morning, we should be asking Him, "God, what do You want from me today?" It doesn't matter what we did yesterday, because today is a new day, a day defined by our relationship with God and not by a routine.

The worship that God desires is not a religious practice. As a pastor, I like it when people come to church, but I don't want them to come to church simply because it's part of their routine. Church is often called a "worship service" for a reason. We view the hymns and music as worship, but the whole service is supposed to be worship. For instance, even while attendees are listening to the sermon, they should be offering God something. They should be thinking about how they can apply what they're learning in the sermon to their daily lives and how they can offer it back to God in worship. That's much richer than a routine; that's being fully engaged in a posture of worship.

I have one more definition for *worship* that I'd like to share with you: "extravagant respect or admiration for or devotion to an object of esteem."[6] This is the definition I like the most because it describes what we see happening around us. We see people worship sports teams like this. We see people worship their spouse or their children like this.

Let's be honest: this is why we're in the trouble we're in. God should be the sole recipient of our most extravagant worship—not another person, an object, or even a political ideology. When we worship someone or something more extravagantly than we worship God, that person or thing has become an idol.

Some of these sports fans and political supporters are more extravagant in their worship than we Christians are in our worship of God. I understand that sometimes we're just tired or we're going through hard times, and we drag ourselves to church in the midst of that struggle. But no matter what we're dealing with, God is still worthy, and He deserves worthy worship—not tired or sinful worship, but extravagant worship. He deserves worthy worship because of who He is.

BE WILLING TO WORSHIP

How, then, do we give God the worthy worship He deserves? First, we must be willing to worship. Worship is an act of the will. When we get into a routine, we may be acting out of our feelings instead of a conscious decision of our will. Back in the day in the Pentecostal church, people would talk about how someone "caught the Holy Ghost." Because of the way that person acted, other people thought that he or she had "caught" something. Whether we catch it or not, we need to know how to tap into the worship inside of us—not just from a feeling, but on purpose. It's not about randomly lucking into an experience, but intentionally embracing God's presence.

Our worship doesn't necessarily need to involve lifting

our hands, dancing, or crying. It can be quiet or even silent. It just needs to come from the heart.

Let's take a look at Genesis 22:1: "After these things God tested Abraham and said to him, 'Abraham!' And he said, 'Here I am.'" Worthy worship is often connected to a test. Sometimes God will call you to worship Him while you are being tested. Remember that worship is about God's worth, not about what you're going through. It's not about you; it's about Him.

When we find ourselves in testing and trying situations, the obvious thing for us to do is to retract our worship. But if everyone going through difficult circumstances were to stop going to church, there wouldn't be anyone at church, because everyone is going through something. Since testing is often a part of worship, if we want to win in life, we must still worship during our tests.

Genesis 22:2 tells us what Abraham's test was: "[God] said, 'Take your son, your only son Isaac, whom you love, and go to the land of Moriah, and offer him there as a burnt offering on one of the mountains of which I shall tell you.'" It's one thing to be tested by the circumstances around you. It's another thing to be tested because you're following God.

In other words, God gives you an instruction, and that instruction is so outlandish that it turns your world upside down. But even when God is the one who seems to be causing you trouble, He is still worthy of your worship. Abraham had waited for so many years for God to give him his promised son, and now God was telling him to sacrifice that son. Can you imagine how shocked and confused Abraham must have felt?

Sometimes what God calls us to do will cost us. There is nothing in Scripture that guarantees us that life is going to be a bowl of cherries. When God calls you, it will test you. His version of winning may not always align with your ideals. It will be hard on you, but He is still worthy of your worship.

The test is to see whether you will continue to worship God even when He gives you an instruction that you really don't like. For example, He may be telling you to stay in your marriage when all you want to do is get a divorce. Staying in that marriage is the last thing you want to do, but He is testing your worship. Tomorrow's victorious marriage may start with today's selfless obedience. Notice, too, that Genesis 22:1 doesn't say that Satan tested Abraham. It says that God tested Abraham.

WORTHY WORSHIP REVEALS WHAT YOU LOVE

Why do we worship to begin with? Worthy worship proves what we value most. This takes us to our second point about worthy worship: it proves what you love. Let's take a look at Genesis 22:3: "So Abraham rose early in the morning, saddled his donkey, and took two of his young men with him, and his son Isaac. And he cut the wood for the burnt offering and arose and went to the place of which God had told him."

This verse doesn't say, "Abraham rose early in the morning and argued with God." It doesn't say that Abraham called his friend on the phone and complained about God's instructions. He just started doing what God had told him to do, and that is why he is considered our father in faith. Sometimes you just have to do what God tells you to do, even when you don't understand.

Even when it doesn't make sense to us, we can trust that God sees the big picture. It may look like our way would be the better way to do things, but God's way is always the right way. We can trust that He is leading us to a victory that only He can see. He is God, and we are not. He is deserving of worthy worship, and by giving Him that worship, we prove that we love Him more than we love our own way of doing things.

Some of us love our own way more than we love God. We're with God as long as He tells us everything we want to hear, but when He tells us something that's outside of our way, we refuse to engage. For example, maybe you're receiving a bonus from your place of employment, and you already know exactly how you're going to spend that money. Then God asks you to give some of that money to the church or to a neighbor who is in need. That was not part of your plan.

Now, obviously, you're an adult and can do what you want with your money. That's not my point. My point is that our obedience is everything. Here's the larger truth I'm trying to convey: doing things your own way is why you always find yourself in the situations that you're in. At some point, you're going to have to trust God and do things His way. Abraham understood that God had brought him this far. He didn't understand what God was doing, but he knew that God still deserved his worship and obedience.

Abraham knew that God had given him a son even though he and his wife, Sarah, were unable to have children up to that point. Because of that, he knew that God knew what He was doing. Abraham saddled his donkey and made the preparations to do what God had told him to do, even though it didn't make sense to him. He chose to trust God.

Let me give you an example from my own life. A few years ago, I worked with a coach who trains ministries in church growth by restructuring their use of social media into a beneficial church marketing tool. He had developed a detailed strategy for my church's social media and marketing teams, but the coaching strategy would cost about three thousand dollars.

My initial thought was that there was no way God was asking me to do this. Over the past few years, I have committed to starting the new year without any debt. I've worked my way down to having one credit card, and at the end of December each year, I pay off whatever remains on that credit card.

Now, I could have funded this church marketing project with money from the church accounts, but I didn't feel like God was telling me to do that. So, I concluded that this project wasn't for me.

Then I heard God tell me, "Do it from your own money." I wasn't even sure if it was God at first, because I didn't have the money to do it. If I did it, it would have to go on my credit card. It was late November at the time, which meant that I would have to pay off three thousand dollars that I hadn't budgeted for by the end of December. I'm not poor, and I don't mind giving generously to ministry initiatives, but like most people who will read this book, I do not have an endless supply of money.

Despite all of this, I became more and more convinced that God was asking me to do this. By faith, I pulled the trigger, and I did it. The next day, I woke up thinking that putting that unbudgeted three thousand dollars on my credit card was just about the stupidest thing I had ever done. Even so, I could feel God asking me to trust Him that this was a winning move.

By the third week of December, that entire unplanned three thousand dollars was paid off, and I had money to spare. Money came in ways I could never have expected and from sources I didn't know I had. God made it clear that if I trust Him and step out, even if it doesn't make sense and it's over my budget, He "is able to do far more abundantly than all that we ask or think" (Ephesians 3:20).

And it didn't stop there. Blessings continued to roll in over the next few months. God knows what He is doing, but you have to have a lifestyle that says you will trust Him with your worship, even if it means doing things that you didn't plan to do.

WORTHY WORSHIP RESULTS IN PROVISION

Let's continue with Genesis 22:4–5: "On the third day Abraham lifted up his eyes and saw the place from afar. Then Abraham said to his young men, 'Stay here with the donkey; I and the boy will go over there and worship and come again to you.'"

It was a three-day journey to reach their destination. Abraham had plenty of opportunities to turn back, but he chose to keep moving forward in obedience to God. God told Abraham to sacrifice his son, to kill his son, yet Abraham told the young men who were with them, "We are going to worship." That sure doesn't sound like worship to me. What did Abraham understand that we don't understand?

Abraham knew that he was undergoing something that was testing his worship, and he believed that both he and his son Isaac would return from that time of worship. That brings us to our third point about worthy worship: it is connected to faith. Your faithfulness is revealed through your worship, and your worship is seen through your faithfulness. If you can see every step on the road ahead, it's not faith, and it probably isn't worthy worship, either.

Sometimes you have to move forward without knowing where you're going. You have to walk blindly. You have to put yourself out there, trusting, believing, and leaning on God. You have to trust that His way is the best way, that His victory is the best victory.

And Abraham took the wood of the burnt offering and laid it on Isaac his son. And he took in his hand the fire and the knife. So they went both of them together. And Isaac said to his father Abraham, "My father!" And he said, "Here I am, my son." He said, "Behold, the fire and the wood, but where is the lamb for a burnt offering?" Abraham said, "God will provide for himself the lamb for a burnt offering, my son." So they went both of them together.
—Genesis 22:6–8

That's the kind of worship I'm talking about, when you can be so bold at that point of testing and obedience that you tell family members that God will provide. You may not know how, where, or when He will provide, but your worship tells you that He is a provider.

Abraham didn't know how God was going to provide, but he knew that God saw him, and he knew that God wasn't going to leave him out there like that. James Cleveland expressed this beautifully: "I've come too far from where I started from. Nobody told me that the road would be easy. I don't believe He brought me this far to leave me."[7]

There is something about the God whom we worship that when we give Him worthy worship, it reminds us that He still comes through. Even in the midnight hour, He still comes through. We may not know how it will happen, but our God will provide. Our God always comes through.

Before Abraham received the son that God had promised him, he spent twenty-five years trusting and believing God (Genesis 12:1–4; 21:5). Now that he had received his promised son, he was determined not to let anything wrestle his son out of his hand. He didn't know how God was going to do it, but he knew that he and his son were going to return from this sacrifice. That type of trust is worship.

What do you need to trust God for at this time? If your worship is worthy, you can look at whatever circumstances you may face and have the faith and the confidence to say, "God will provide."

Let's examine Abraham further. We've shown how he declared that God would provide, and we've connected that kind of faithful trust to worthy worship. Yet the question remains: Did God come through?

Genesis 22:11–14 says:

> But the angel of the LORD called to him from heaven and said, "Abraham, Abraham!" And he said, "Here I am." He said, "Do not lay your hand on the boy or do anything to him, for now I know that you fear God, seeing you have not withheld your son, your only son, from me." And Abraham lifted up his eyes and looked, and behold, behind him was a ram, caught in a thicket by his horns. And Abraham went and took the ram and offered it up as a burnt offering instead of his son. So Abraham called the name of that place, "The LORD will provide"; as it is said to this day, "On the mount of the LORD it shall be provided."

In the original Hebrew of verse 14, Abraham refers to God as Jehovah Jireh, which means that God sees and, because of what He sees, God provides.[8] How will you get over the loss of a loved one? God will provide. How are you going to pay your bills? God will provide. How are you going to fix your children, mend your relationships, and hold on to your job? God will provide. That is our fourth point about worthy worship. Worthy worship results in provision because it shifts us into the spiritual.

WORTHY WORSHIP SHIFTS YOU
INTO THE SPIRITUAL

Worthy worship shifts us from the natural to the spiritual. This is the shift that Jesus spoke to the Samaritan woman about, the shift that is coming. The natural and the spiritual operate on parallel planes. In other words, they operate next to each other. When you're operating in the natural, there are things that shift you over to the spiritual, to the supernatural, and when you're operating in the spiritual and supernatural, there are things that shift you over to the natural.

In John 4:23, Jesus said, "But the hour is coming, and is now here, when the true worshipers will worship the Father in spirit and truth, for the Father is seeking such people to worship him." The hour has come, and it is here for us. If there are true worshipers, then that means there are also false worshipers. The true worshipers will worship in spirit and truth.

Worship is about more than just music or attending church; it's a lifestyle. It is spirit, and it is truth. It is victory. It's more than the particulars, and it's more than the routine. It's more than religion. What are you doing for God? Are you just doing what everyone else does, or do you actually have a personal relationship with Him? Stop getting caught up in a routine and start worshiping God in spirit and in truth.

You need to be able to talk to God for yourself. A pastor can preach to you and teach you, but he can't get you into heaven. You need to have your own relationship with God and pray and worship for yourself. You can't do it all on Sunday morning. Worthy worship is a lifestyle, a spiritual lifestyle that leads to spiritual victories.

WORTHY WORSHIP SENDS THE DEVIL PACKING

We also worship so that we can prove not only to ourselves, but also to the devil, what is most valuable to us. Sometimes when you tell the devil to get out of your life, he keeps hanging around because he doesn't see you worshiping God. He doesn't see you valuing God, so he doesn't trust your words. The devil doesn't believe that God will provide for you, because he doesn't see you worshiping God, so he's willing to take his chances with you.

Many times, the devil beats you to the punch and wears you out, leaving you to wonder why God didn't step in and fix things for you. But once you worship God, it does something to you. Your worship is for Him, but it does something to you because you realize that the God you are worshiping is connected to you.

First John 4:4 puts it this way: "Little children, you are from God and have overcome them, for he who is in you is greater than he who is in the world." When I worship God, something happens to me, like when Clark Kent steps into the phone booth and becomes Superman. When I step into my prayer closet, I may be sick, but when I step out, I step out healed because I am worshiping God and I value Him the most.

When I place a high value on God, I simultaneously realize

that He has placed a high value on me. He has put His breath in my body, and He has paid for all of my sins with His blood. When I die, I will join Him in heaven. That devil who keeps hounding me was kicked out of heaven, but heaven is my final destination. It sounds like I'm more important than Satan, doesn't it? If the devil wants to fight me, I say bring it on, because I've already won in Christ. My worship reminds me of my victory. There is no losing for those who are in Christ!

The same is true for you, but you won't know that unless you worship. Just take a moment to be with God. Put down your phone, turn off the TV, and block out any distractions. Consider stepping outside and appreciating His creation. Before you go to bed at night, when the house is quiet, spend some time worshiping the Lord. Whatever you do and however you do it, take a moment to thank God for simply being who He is. When you give God a moment in time, He steps into that moment, and when He steps into a moment, He does amazing things.

WORTHY WORSHIP INCREASES OUR VALUE

We worship because it reveals what we value most, and it also increases our value. I've learned that it's hard to have low self-esteem if you are worshiping God properly. We all have things about us that we don't like. Some of those things we can change, and some of them we can't. But when we start embracing God and worshiping Him, we realize that we are His vessels. We stop talking down to ourselves, because when we talk down to ourselves, we're talking about our God. We're talking about His creation.

For example, I refuse to be anyone's ugly anymore. I don't know who they're talking to or who they're looking at, but I'm not ugly. I'm not going to be anyone's ugly anymore, and I'm not going to be anyone's stupid, either. I use these arbitrary examples, but you can fill in the blank with any kind of negative talk that has come your way. You need to set some boundaries and stop letting other people talk to you however they want. That means putting some boundaries on what you say to yourself as well.

You are a child of God, and yes, you look good. Maybe other people disagree, but your focus isn't on Hollywood's standards of beauty or what other people think. It's on what God thinks, and when God made you, He said it was good. You are good and you are somebody because of God. You are "fearfully and wonderfully made" (Psalm 139:14). We all have issues that we struggle with in our lives, but why do we need to focus on that? Let's focus on God and His goodness instead.

Sometimes we act like the little things are such a big deal. Maybe you're fixated on the fact that you have "only" a GED and not a college degree. That happened years ago. Think about how far you've made it with "just" a GED. Instead of focusing on the past and crying about it, why don't you praise God for how far He has brought you? We tend to focus on the wrong things, but when we begin to worship God, all the right things start to come into focus.

WORTHY WORSHIP ILLUMINATES
YOUR IGNORANCE

Worthy worship reveals the extent of our ignorance. When we begin to put God before ourselves, it shows us the areas in our lives where we are ignorant of God as well as the areas where we have been ignoring Him intentionally. Worship helps us to understand where we are failing God by shining a light on those areas so that we can offer them to Him.

Let's take a look at John 4:19–20: "The woman said to him, 'Sir, I perceive that you are a prophet. Our fathers worshiped on this mountain, but you say that in Jerusalem is the place where people ought to worship.'" In these verses, a Samaritan woman whom Jesus met at a well was asking Him questions about worship. It's a familiar story from Scripture. Jesus had already told her that she'd had five husbands and that the man she was currently with wasn't her husband (John 4:16–18), which is why she recognized Him as a prophet. But He wasn't finished dealing with her.

The Samaritan woman had some questions for Jesus about the right way to worship. The reason that we need to grow beyond our ignorance is that there are people out there who want to reach out to God but are confused. We need to be able to respond to their confusion and their doubts, but if we aren't worshiping God ourselves, we can't help anyone else.

Let's see how Jesus responded to the Samaritan woman's

questions in John 4:21–22: "Jesus said to her, 'Woman, believe me, the hour is coming when neither on this mountain nor in Jerusalem will you worship the Father. You worship what you do not know; we worship what we know, for salvation is from the Jews.'" He told her that she was worshiping out of ignorance and that a time was coming when worship would not be about the particulars or the routine.

I believe that one of the reasons God has allowed us to experience the COVID-19 pandemic is because there is a lot of ignorance in the church. There's a lot of fussing and fighting, and much of it is over things that don't even mean anything. God has made it clear to us that we're worshiping something we don't even know and that a shift is coming. It will no longer be about denominations and popes, bishops and pastors, and all the man-made particulars. God is shaking that stuff up and making sure that He is the main focus of His church, and we'd better grab hold of Him above anything else.

You can't base your worship on random things you read on the internet or solely on things that other people tell you. You need to have your own connection with God and be able to use prayer and His Word to discern the truth yourself. It doesn't matter how good it sounds; if it doesn't feel right in your spirit, it's not right. That goes for what your pastor teaches you as well. I expect the members of my congregation to have individual relationships with God that are so strong that they can correct me if I need it and keep me from leading them in the wrong direction. If we hang on to God, He will see us through our ignorance and disciple us in the knowledge of Him.

WORTHY WORSHIP IS PROACTIVE

Worthy worship forces us to be proactive rather than reactive. Praise is reactive. If someone gives you something, you react to the gift by thanking that person. You can't thank someone for giving you something until he or she gives it to you. Worship, on the other hand, is proactive. Praise is based on what God does, but worship is based on who He is. Even when God doesn't appear to be doing anything, He is still worthy of worship because He is still God.

We can praise God when we have money in the bank and when we're in good health. We can praise Him when things are good in our marriage and when things are going smoothly in our children's lives. But what about when we're struggling to make ends meet and our relationships are in shambles? What about when our health is poor, our anxiety is spiraling out of control, and our sleep is disrupted by nightmares or insomnia?

Worship says that even in states such as these, we should still give God what He deserves. We don't have to wait for Him to bring us out of the situation. We can and should worship Him right where we are. We don't wait until the battle is over; we shout right now because we know that He is able, even if He hasn't done it yet.

Like Shadrach, Meshach, and Abednego when they were confronted with the fiery furnace for refusing to bow down to King Nebuchadnezzar's golden image (Daniel 3), we worship God because we know that He is able to deliver us. Our children may be dealing with difficulties, but we know that God is able to bring them out of those difficulties. Our physical and mental health may be deteriorating, but we know that God is able to bring us out of that. We worship Him proactively. Even if He chooses not to deliver us from a certain situation in the way we want, it doesn't change our worship.

Some of us are spoiled because of the ways God has previously been good to us. When He starts doing a new thing in a different way, it throws some of us off. In my city, everything was good as long as we had our major industries. When those industries packed up and left, people had to find other ways to make ends meet, and some started to think that maybe God wasn't so good after all. But God is still good, even in the middle of an economic downturn. He is still good in the middle of a divorce, and He is still good in the middle of a pandemic. God is still good because God is still God.

Worthy worship does not withhold worship based on our circumstances, as we see in Psalm 34:1–3:

I will bless the LORD at all times; his praise shall continually be in my mouth. My soul makes its boast in the LORD; let the humble hear and be glad. Oh, magnify the LORD with me, and let us exalt his name together!

David wrote those verses while he was hiding in a cave from King Saul, who was trying to kill him. David had just faked insanity in order to escape the clutches of Achish, the king of Gath (1 Samuel 21). Everyone who was in debt, in distress, or bitter had come to join him in his cave (1 Samuel 22). He had nothing, yet he was able to write those words: "I will bless the LORD at all times" (Psalm 34:1). When times are bad, we're still blessing God, because it's not about praise; it's about worship.

David had been promised a kingdom. He had been anointed to be king, yet there he was, stuck in a cave. Even in those circumstances, he still worshiped God. Some of the things that have been promised to you may not seem like they're even close to being fulfilled, but your worship should communicate that it doesn't make a difference. Even if you have to wait until your deathbed for those promises to be fulfilled, you'll still give God praise and glory.

Your worship should communicate that you're always glad to come to church, read your Bible, and talk to God, even if He never does another thing for you, because you know that He isn't Santa Claus or a magic genie. He is God, and He doesn't have to do everything you want Him to do. What He did on Calvary is all you really need. Simply put, as long as He is God, He is worthy. When you have that mindset, unexpected things begin to happen. God will do what you thought you didn't want Him to do, and He will do it so well that you'll realize you did want Him to do it all along.

For example, I never considered being a pastor, but when God presented me with the opportunity, I discovered that I really did want to be a pastor and that I enjoyed the work.

Everything He took me through up to that point had prepared me to do what He has me doing today. I didn't necessarily like that preparation—I've been through some tough stuff—but I'm so grateful for it. God knows what He is doing. That's what makes Him God, and that's what makes Him worthy.

WORTHY WORSHIP CAN HAPPEN
EVEN IN THE WILDERNESS

Afterward Moses and Aaron went and said to Pharaoh, "Thus says the LORD, the God of Israel, 'Let my people go, that they may hold a feast to me in the wilderness.'"
—Exodus 5:1

When we read this verse, we tend to focus on how God determined to free His people from slavery. Did you notice the key reason why He wanted to liberate the Israelites? So that they could worship Him—and not just anywhere, but in the wilderness, a place of hardship. In other words, God is still worthy of being celebrated when you're going through the tough stuff. God didn't want His people to worship Him in bondage, but they didn't go right from captivity to the promised land. They had to journey through the wilderness first, and this was not an excuse not to worship.

Do you find that you can worship God when you're in a dry place? What about when you're in a dark, uncertain, or anxious place? Would you worship Him if you couldn't pay your bills? Do you worship Him when you aren't getting along with your colleagues or your boss seems to have it out for you? Can you worship God in the wilderness? Wilderness worship shows that you trust Him. Worshiping God victoriously in difficult circumstances and offering Him praise shows that you haven't put your faith in unworthy places.

Besides, it makes no sense to deny God worthy worship during our times in the wilderness, because the wilderness is often part of God's plan for our lives. Not every trial we go through is from the devil! Too often, we feel like we should go directly to the promised land once God sets us free from a place of bondage. On the contrary, I've found that there is usually a struggle after God sets us free from something, because the wilderness helps to draw out the remnants of Egypt, the parts that remain from our lives before God freed us. We may retain a lot of the world in us, even after He saves us, but the wilderness can be a place to recognize this and to shed more completely our old ways of thinking.

Continue to worship God in the wilderness, where the struggles are only temporary and are often intended for your benefit. At one point in my life, God was anointing and using me to see people delivered miraculously in out-of-state revivals. Then I'd come back home to a job as a janitor and would be cleaning toilets, because He knew that I could learn some things about humility that way. He expected me to worship Him through it all.

If you're not convinced that God would send you into the wilderness on purpose, remember that He also ordained for

Jesus, His Son, to go into the wilderness: "And Jesus, full of the Holy Spirit, returned from the Jordan and was led by the Spirit in the wilderness for forty days, being tempted by the devil" (Luke 4:1–2). There Jesus showed us that worthy worship in the wilderness requires standing firm on the Word, even and especially when you're weak, for "man shall not live by bread alone" (Luke 4:4). Satan tried to tempt Jesus with quicker, easier paths, but He rejected Satan's temptations on the solid ground of Scripture.

Despite the difficulties of the wilderness, it's easy to walk away from Satan's shortcuts when you can see all of the strings attached. The perspective you gain in the wilderness allows you to see Satan's temptations for what they really are: lies to subvert your purpose.

When you truly worship God in the wilderness, the devil can't defeat you. Christ has already won the victory. When you cling to that truth, the devil will have to give up, back off, and regroup (Luke 4:13). God designed our wilderness worship to be a slap in Satan's face! Knowing this, we have no reason to fear either the devil or the wilderness.

That said, in our eagerness to defeat Satan, let's not stray far from Jesus' example. Jesus stayed solely within the confines of God's Word. When Satan tried to quote Scripture to get Jesus to jump from a high place to prove that He was the Son of God, Jesus refused (Luke 4:9–12). Jesus recognized the difference between faith and foolishness. Likewise, we shouldn't mistake reckless worship for wilderness worship. Recklessness is buying a wedding dress and booking the venue before you're even dating anyone. It's overextending yourself in careless debts and declaring that "God will provide." Some people claim to be operating in faith and worshiping God when they handle snakes or when they refuse to wear a protective mask in a crowd during a pandemic. We should look to Jesus' response to Satan in Scripture: "You shall not put the Lord your God to the test" (Luke 4:12). Make sure that you're not tempting God with your bad choices and then calling it worship!

Real, worthy wilderness worship exalts Jesus Christ by acknowledging our complete dependence on Him and what He did for us on the cross for our salvation. Wilderness worship shows that we know we can trust God, who knows what He is doing and always acts in a deliberate, orderly way on our behalf. He knows each of us, no matter where we find ourselves. When we are on His side, we will always win.

HOW TO REMAIN IN A WORSHIP MINDSET

Deuteronomy 11:18–19 states, "You shall therefore lay up these words of mine in your heart and in your soul, and you shall bind them as a sign on your hand, and they shall be as frontlets between your eyes. You shall teach them to your children, talking of them when you are sitting in your house, and when you are walking by the way, and when you lie down, and when you rise."

This is what helps us to stay in this worship mindset, even in the wilderness. It's hard not to worship God when you have His Word in your mind and in your heart and you're talking about it with your children—not just your physical children, but your spiritual children as well, the people whom you mentor and disciple, and others within your sphere of influence.

Let's continue with Deuteronomy 11:20: "You shall write them on the doorposts of your house and on your gates." That's something you can do very easily in your own home. Take some index cards and write on them Bible verses that are particularly meaningful to you. Stick the cards on your bathroom mirror so that when you're brushing your teeth, you'll look up and be reminded that you can do anything through Christ, who strengthens you (Philippians 4:13). Put the Bible verses up in various places throughout your house so that you will be reminded of God and His Word.

Jot down scriptures digitally in the notes on your smart phone or record your own voice speaking God's Word. Play videos from the internet that feature God's Word set to music. Listen to positive, faith-filled music when you're in the car.

Hang up pictures that remind you of the things of God so that when you're going through dark times, you can look up and remember that He has brought you "into his marvelous light" (1 Peter 2:9). Some people who struggle with addiction have the serenity prayer on display in their homes. They keep that prayer before their eyes to remind them that God is with them in their struggles. If you have everything but God before your eyes, you are going to have a hard time giving Him worthy worship.

We have TV, social media, and all kinds of media streaming services to occupy our time. We had better add

God in there somewhere, or we will be overcome by the things of this world. Instead of spending all your time on Facebook, consider putting your face in His book.

FIVE FORMS OF WORTHY WORSHIP

Going to church on Sunday is like filling up at the gas station. You get filled up for what you're going to face during the upcoming week, but once you're filled up, you have to start driving. You're going to run out of spiritual fuel during the week, probably multiple times, so you need to know how to worship on your own so that you can replenish your tank.

Let's take a look at five forms of worthy worship. The first is teaching and preaching. Yes, they are forms of worship, and it's your responsibility to access teaching and preaching beyond what you're receiving at church. It's as simple as listening to Christian radio or watching sermons from reputable preachers online. If you're a lazy Christian in this day and age and you're going unfed spiritually, it's no one's fault but your own. There are so many avenues for you to be taught and for you to hear God.

In 1 Corinthians 4:17, Paul stated, "That is why I sent you Timothy, my beloved and faithful child in the Lord, to remind you of my ways in Christ, as I teach them everywhere in every church." Learning about Christ and His ways is a form of worthy worship.

The second form of worthy worship is singing. It doesn't matter if you don't sound like a professional; everyone and anyone can sing. Ephesians 5:19 encourages us to address "one another in psalms and hymns and spiritual songs, singing and making melody to the Lord with your heart." That doesn't necessarily mean that we communicate with each other by singing, but that we have a joyful spirit.

Sometimes you wake up with a song in your spirit. It puts a pep in your step and directs your day. You shouldn't be drunk with wine to the point where you are being controlled by wine (Ephesians 5:18). Instead, you should be controlled by the songs of the Lord and your worship of Him. You can sing at home and in your car, and you can reflect on the lyrics and think about what they mean. All of that is part of worthy worship.

The third form of worthy worship is prayer. Acts 12:5 tells us, "So Peter was kept in prison, but earnest prayer for him was made to God by the church." The church was being persecuted, and Peter had been locked up in prison, but the saints of God were praying for his release. The Bible also tells us that God restored Job's fortunes after he prayed for his friends (Job 42:10). When you pray for other people, that is worthy worship.

The fourth form of worthy worship is taking a collection. In 1 Corinthians 16:1-2, Paul wrote, "Now concerning the collection for the saints: as I directed the churches of Galatia, so you also are to do. On the first day of every week, each of you is to put something aside and store it up, as he may prosper, so that there will be no collecting when I come."

At the beginning of the week, you should be setting something aside. Before you come to church, you should already plan on giving to God. That amount should not decrease once God begins tugging on your heart and provoking generosity; it should only increase. The amount starts changing because, through worship, God is changing you. If you think that He is asking you to give less, you probably aren't hearing Him right, or you fail to see giving as an act of worship.

Now, no pastor should be trying to pressure you or manipulate you into giving money to the church. That isn't of God. Your giving is something that is to be decided between you and God as an outpouring of worthy worship.

The fifth and final form of worthy worship is the Lord's supper, which is also known as communion. Paul told us in 1 Corinthians 11:23–26:

> For I received from the Lord what I also delivered to you, that the Lord Jesus on the night when he was betrayed took bread, and when he had given thanks, he broke it, and said, "This is my body, which is for you. Do this in remembrance of me." In the same way also he took the cup, after supper, saying, "This cup is the new covenant in my blood. Do this, as often as you drink it, in remembrance of me." For as often as you eat this bread and drink the cup, you proclaim the Lord's death until he comes.

Participating in the Lord's supper puts us in a position of remembering Jesus and the victory He has achieved for us. We remember the fact that He died for our sins, and we are filled with gratitude as we offer Him worthy worship in this way.

GIVE GOD WHAT HE DESERVES

Worship is more than a routine or a ritual; it's a lifestyle. God deserves not just worship, but worthy worship because of who He is. No matter what our circumstances may be, no matter what we may be going through, God will always deserve worthy worship, because He never changes.

To give Him worthy worship, we must first be willing to worship. Worthy worship proves what we love, and it results in God's provision. It sends the devil packing, and it increases our value. Worthy worship is proactive, not reactive. It identifies our ignorance and shifts us from the natural to the spiritual.

We were made for worship, so if we don't worship God, we will worship someone or something else. We can offer Him worthy worship by listening to preaching and teaching, by singing, by praying, by giving, and by taking communion.

Let us endeavor to give our worthy God the honor that is due His name. Regardless of the season or circumstances we find ourselves in, He is always worthy, and we should give Him worthy worship.

Chapter One Questions

Question: In your own words, what is worship that is worthy of God? Do you worship Him with that kind of worship?

_____

_____

_____

_____

_____

_____

_____

_____

_____

_____

_____

_____

Question: Is your worship limited to singing songs in a church service? How do you worship God with your life?

_____

_____

_____

_____

_____

_____

_____

_____

_____

_____

Question: Describe a time when you had to trust and worship God even when you didn't know what the outcome would be. How did God meet you in that situation? What can you learn from that situation of worship and how can you apply it moving forward? What do you need to trust God for at this time?

_____

_____

_____

_____

_____

_____

_____

_____

_____

_____

_____

Question: In what area of life is the devil tempting or distracting you? How can you use worship to send the devil packing?

_____

_____

_____

_____

_____

_____

_____

_____

_____

_____

Question: How can worshiping God impact your self-worth? Describe a time when God used worship to reveal the truth to you.

_____

_____

_____

_____

_____

_____

_____

_____

_____

_____

_____

_____

Question: Do you struggle to worship God when you are experiencing difficulties in your life? Why or why not? Have you ever experienced a season of needing to worship God even when you felt like you were in the wilderness? What did you learn through that experience?

_____

_____

_____

_____

_____

_____

_____

_____

_____

_____

_____

_____

Question: Which of the five forms of worthy worship are currently active in your life? Which of the five do you struggle with most? How can you begin pursuing that area of worship?

_____

_____

_____

_____

_____

_____

_____

_____

_____

_____

_____

_____

Action: Worship proves what you love. In a notebook or journal, create a list of your behaviors that reveal what you are invested in. Where do you spend your time, your focus, your energy, your resources, etc.? Keep track of these things and assess what you are worshiping with your life. Is your life in alignment with a heart set on worshiping God?

Chapter One Notes

_____

_____

_____

_____

_____

_____

_____

_____

_____

_____

_____

_____

_____

_____

_____

Wired Worship

So far, we've learned that we need to offer God a better worship, a more worthy worship, than what we have been offering Him. We need to give Him worship that shows respect for who He is. Even though, as we discussed in the previous chapter, we were created to worship, there are some obstacles within us that get in the way of that.

Here's a powerful truth that I want you to let sink in: we are wired for worship, but we can't worship how we're wired. Because of Adam and Eve's failure in the Garden of Eden (Genesis 3), we have been rewired outside of the way God originally wired us. We were created in God's image, and He breathed His breath into us (Genesis 1:26–27; 2:7). We are wired to worship our Creator, but because of the fall of man and because we have this thing called the flesh, we have to be careful not to worship how we have been rewired.

In other words, we are not everything that we're supposed to be, because we live in a fallen world. In our fallen state, we have a tendency to put things above God and worship those things the way we should be worshiping God. We were originally wired for godly worship (past tense in heaven), but we were rewired for worldly worship (present tense on earth). Our tendency to worship worldly things can get in the way of our worship of God.

Psalm 51:5 does a good job of explaining this: "Behold, I was brought forth in iniquity, and in sin did my mother conceive me." The reason that we can't always worship in the way we were originally wired is because of the fall of man. We were born in sin. David wrote this verse after he had sinned with Bathsheba. He repented before the Lord and acknowledged that he was born a mess.

In Romans 7:18, Paul wrote, "For I know that nothing good dwells in me, that is, in my flesh. For I have the desire to do what is right, but not the ability to carry it out." Essentially, we have dual natures competing inside of us, the nature of the Spirit and the nature of the flesh. Because we live in a fleshly realm, we are tempted to worship from the wiring of our flesh instead of the wiring of the Spirit.

Because of Adam, our wiring is faulty. We have been rewired again through Christ so that we desire to worship God and are able to do so, but we still have a tendency to worship from our old wiring. When we come out of ungodly behaviors and lifestyles and into the things of God, sometimes the old man wants to regain control. If you're in the habit of cussing out other people while driving, that tendency doesn't automatically disappear when you come to Christ. That old spirit isn't totally dead, and it likes to rise up again.

The problem is that we try to create a space for our flesh when we should be creating a space for our God. We're all only human, but we often worship our humanness instead of worshiping the spirituality that God is trying to develop in us. Yes, deliverance and sanctification are a journey, but we have to start focusing on and functioning from our deliverance and sanctification rather than our flesh.

When we worship from our old wiring, from our flesh, we may think that the church service should go the way we want it to go. We assume that everything should be centered around us. In other words, if you want me to praise God, then you'd better sing my favorite songs. Do you want me to give God glory? You'd better preach my kind of sermon.

Listen to me: if God woke you up this morning and there is breath in your body, He deserves your worship, regardless of who's preaching or what songs are being sung. There's nothing inherently wrong with having your preferences, but God is deserving of your praise no matter what. Stop coming to church for people—the worship singers, the pastor, even yourself—and start coming to church for God.

Let me reiterate, even though we are wired for worship, we need to be careful not to worship in the way we are wired, because we've got some stuff in us that is not altogether lovely. God is working on us, but that's no excuse to get stuck in our flesh and worship from our flesh. For example, you may not always feel like giving to your local church, but giving isn't supposed to be based on your feelings. We give because we are worshiping God. Whether it requires us to give of our time, our talents, or our treasure, we need to do it because we're worshiping from the Spirit, which prompts generosity, not from the flesh, which encourages stinginess.

Remember what Jesus said in John 4:24: "God is spirit, and those who worship him must worship in spirit and truth." Notice how He didn't say spirit, truth, and sometimes the flesh. We all need to work on that, because worshiping with a Spirit-rewired perspective is how we win in life.

NO OTHER GODS BEFORE HIM

Deuteronomy 11:16 tells us, "Take care lest your heart be deceived, and you turn aside and serve other gods and worship them." This is another important reason why we worship God. We were created to worship, but this worthy worship we are speaking of is to be given to God only. If we don't worship God first and foremost, our hearts will shift, and we will worship something or someone else. As I explained in Chapter One, worship reveals whom or what we love.

That's why, years ago, you would see people passing out at concerts for Michael Jackson or the Beatles like someone just laid hands on them at an altar call. We are made to worship something, and if you don't know what to worship, you'll worship the wrong thing. I don't know about you, but I don't want any man or material thing taking the place of God in my life. I don't want a sports team, a car, a house, or a job to take God's place in my life. If I don't worship Him, I'm going to worship something else.

Simply put, worshiping out of our old, fleshly desires tempts us to worship something else above God. Whenever we worship from the flesh, there is a significant temptation to put things above and over our God. When God wakes us up in the morning and asks us to pray, we are considerably less excited about that than, say, a new car. The main reason for this is that God is invisible to our eyes, whereas we can see the things that we are tempted to worship instead of Him.

God said:

> *You shall have no other gods before me. You shall not make for yourself a carved image, or any likeness of anything that is in heaven above, or that is in the earth beneath, or that is in the water under the earth. You shall not bow down to them or serve them, for I the LORD your God am a jealous God....*
>
> **—Exodus 20:3–5**

Because we are no longer operating under the Old Testament and we do not always experience automatic punishments when we disobey God, we tend to put Him on the back burner. We act like everything else is more important than God, but God makes it clear that we should have no other gods before Him. He is a jealous God, and He is right to be jealous over us, because He created us and He purchased us with His own blood.

If anyone has a right to you, it's God. If anyone has a right to your time, it's God. Worship is not always easy. Sometimes it requires us to sacrifice, but if anyone deserves a sacrifice of worship, it's God. Even so, we continue to put things above

Him. I'm not talking about people out in the world; they don't know any better. I'm talking about us, the people of God. We should know better.

In this day and age, we're busier than we've ever been before. There's always something to do. But God is too worthy to be put on the back burner, to be pushed aside and paid attention to later. Talk to Him whenever you have the opportunity—in the car, at the store, during your break at work. Do not dishonor Him by ignoring Him. He is worthy of our worship, and He has offered us relationship with Him. Let's cherish this love relationship by keeping Him as our priority.

How Women Put Relationships Above God

In addition to being wired for worship, we are wired for relationship. Unfortunately, we tend to place human relationships above God, and that often gets in the way of His will for us. I think that we'll be better equipped to ward off temptation if we first understand how women and men are wired for relationships in their flesh and what the Bible has to say about all of this.

Let's begin with women's faulty wiring. In Genesis 3:16, God told Eve how she would be punished for her disobedience in the Garden of Eden: "To the woman he said, 'I will surely multiply your pain in childbearing; in pain you shall bring forth children. Your desire shall be contrary to your husband, but he shall rule over you.'"

We're going to focus on the second half of this verse.

Scholars have two different interpretations of what God was saying here. Some believe it means that the wife will desire to control her husband.[9] Part of the faulty wiring of women is that they can love to be in control. When you worship from that place, it's difficult to trust God to handle key relationships in your life, because you're used to running the show or manipulating situations for desired outcomes. That's part of the fall for women, and it needs to be balanced properly.

I can't tell you how many women have complained to me about the husbands they are trying to control. They saw all the red flags, but they thought that they could change their husbands. They thought that they could fix their husbands and control them, then everything would be just fine. But it didn't work. Now things are a mess, and they want their pastor to counsel them out of it. I can't counsel them out of that issue, because they worshiped their flesh, their faulty wiring. They thought that they could fix everything with manipulation and control.

That's something that some women need to learn to dial back. It's hard to trust God if you always need to have your hand in everything. He will fix things for us, but we may need to get our hands out of it first. Since my message here is for women readers, allow me to add that this includes nagging. No one, no matter how good a person he or she is, responds well to nagging. You can trust God to deal with someone, or you can nag that person to death. Nagging isn't going to produce lasting change, so you may as well trust God instead. You need to let go and let God.

Obviously, men, too, often find themselves in situations where the need for control rears its ugly head. I'm addressing women in particular here because of the curse on women that their "desire shall be contrary to" their husbands (Genesis 3:16), which, again, some scholars believe manifests in a need for control.[10]

There is another interpretation of the second half of Genesis 3:16, which is clearer when we look at the verse in another translation: "To the woman he said, 'I will make your pains in childbearing very severe; with painful labor you will give birth to children. Your desire will be for your husband, and he will rule over you'" (NIV). Some scholars believe that the second half of this verse refers to a desire for companionship, a desire so strong that a woman is willing to be ruled by her husband.[11]

I want to speak to single women in particular here. For some of you, even though God has done so much for you, you can have an attitude with Him simply because you don't have someone to celebrate special days like Valentine's Day with. You struggle with envy and find it hard to praise God when someone else gets married. God can bless you in your career and give you a house and a car, but you can't be bothered to thank Him, because He hasn't given you a man.

I'm not saying that you shouldn't have a husband, but when a woman desires companionship too much, it can cause her to get ahead of God. It can cause her to treat God poorly because she doesn't have what some other women have. It can cause her to idolize the hope of a natural relationship above the reality of her current connection to God, her

Creator.

Loneliness is not the worst thing. Sometimes your singleness and your loneliness are a blessing because, contrary to what romantic movies and novels tell you, there is not a man in this world who can complete you. Only Jesus can do that.

Let me be clear: there's nothing wrong with wanting to have somebody. It's even okay to be honest with God about that, but don't let it drive your worship. If you worship from that desire, then you could have an issue on every holiday that you don't have a man.

Don't allow yourself to get to a point where you can't praise God when your friend gets married and you're still single. Your time will come. If marriage is the desire of your heart, I believe that God will give you that desire as long as you aren't placing it above Him.

What happens when you place this desire above God? For instance, maybe you do have a man, but he's no good. He won't partner with you. He abuses you, he won't come to church with you, he takes all your money, and he refuses to get a job. He constantly does you wrong, but you won't let him go, because you don't want to be lonely. You don't have a real relationship; you just have someone in your life who's comfortable with taking advantage of you.

A woman can want a man in her life so badly that she's willing to be violated and done wrong. You are the apple of God's eye, but you choose to settle because you don't want to be alone. That is an example of operating out of your faulty wiring. I don't want any woman to settle for being unequally yoked (2 Corinthians 6:14). A cheap Valentine's Day card from Walmart isn't worth the hell you will go through with a man who consistently does you wrong.

The reason my wife and I have been married for more than twenty-two years is that we did it the right way. We pursued our relationship God's way and in His timing. I'm not trying to beat anyone up here or make anyone feel bad for past choices. I just want you to understand that your faulty wires can lead you to make choices that may have consequences for the rest of your life. It's not worth it. It's best to wait on God, because His plan is the best plan.

HOW MEN PUT RELATIONSHIPS ABOVE GOD

Men certainly have faulty wires, too. There are so many ways in which our wiring is faulty, but I want to focus specifically on the issue of lust. I will center on married men, but these truths about lust are equally applicable to single men. Men have something wired into us that can lead us to succumb to our physical desire for women. After we have hunted a particular woman and succeeded in establishing a relationship with her, we have a tendency to give into other women's seduction if we worship from those wires.

Great men have fallen because of lust. Proverbs 5:23 has this to say about an adulterous man: "He dies for lack of discipline, and because of his great folly he is led astray." We men get ourselves into a whole lot of trouble because of our lack of discipline.

Proverbs 6:25 warns the man who is considering

committing adultery, "Do not desire her beauty in your heart, and do not let her capture you with her eyelashes." You're going to come across beautiful women in your life who are not your wife, and this verse makes it clear that you should not allow a desire for these women to take root in your heart. Once lust gets into your heart, it will drive you into folly, even if you're saved.

Men are visual creatures, but we need to recognize when we're looking inappropriately. We need to recognize when lust is taking root in our hearts. If we don't pay attention to these things, we'll find ourselves operating out of our faulty wiring and making choices that dishonor God and our wives. We will be ruled by our flesh instead of the Spirit.

I'm not addressing men in the world. My focus is mainly on men in the church. If we are not careful and we give too much credence to our flesh, we will worship from it and will do things that we shouldn't be doing. We will follow paths that we shouldn't be following.

In the book of Proverbs, Solomon told the story of a young man who was tempted by his desire for a woman. Let's take a look at Proverbs 7:6–7: "For at the window of my house I have looked out through my lattice, and I have seen among the simple, I have perceived among the youths, a young man lacking sense." It's important to understand that the spirit of youth is a spirit of being unwise. A person can be old and still be functioning out of a youthful mind and spirit. There's nothing worse than an old fool. We can understand why a young person might be foolish and unwise, but an older person should be wiser and know better.

Proverbs 7:8–10, 13–15 continues:

...passing along the street near her corner, taking the road to her house in the twilight, in the evening, at the time of night and darkness.

And behold, the woman meets him, dressed as a prostitute, wily of heart. ... She seizes him and kisses him, and with bold face she says to him, "I had to offer sacrifices, and today I have paid my vows; so now I have come out to meet you, to seek you eagerly, and I have found you."

This woman was talking about sacrifices and vows. She was a religious woman. But even though she was making sacrifices at the temple like God's law required, her heart was filled with evil intentions. Not everyone who's sitting in church has been delivered. As we've discussed, if a woman is functioning out of her faulty wiring, she may not care if a man is married or not. She just wants a man, and a woman who wants a man has a way of drawing him toward her. Men need to recognize when they are being seduced. If a man doesn't have discipline, he will function out of his faulty wiring and ruin everything.

The woman continued her seductive speech in Proverbs 7:16–17: "I have spread my couch with coverings, colored linens from Egyptian linen; I have perfumed my bed with myrrh, aloes, and cinnamon." Not only was this woman looking good, but she was also speaking pretty good.

I'd like to pause and interject some marital wisdom here. There is no excuse for a married man to fail. That is entirely on him. However, may I add, a wife should not send her husband out hungry for praise, respect, and intimacy, because there will always be another woman willing to feed him. It should not be the case that another woman is telling him how wonderful he is and how handsome he is and he's never hearing anything like that at home.

Even in natural terms, if a man's wife isn't packing him a lunch to tide him over, a woman at his job may start slipping him food. It's still the husband's fault, but I admonish wives to guard this area because there may be a woman out there somewhere with crafty intent. All of this applies similarly to husbands who leave their wives vulnerable to outside temptation.

The woman concluded her speech in Proverbs 7:18–20:

> Come, let us take our fill of love till morning; let us delight ourselves with love. For my husband is not at home; he has gone on a long journey; he took a bag of money with him; at full moon he will come home.

This was no accidental encounter. She didn't "fall into sin." She had planned this, and she knew what she was doing. Even though the woman had a husband, she knew that this young man was unwise and that she could draw him in.

Men need to be careful of the conversations they have, both in person and online. It used to be that if you wanted to have an affair, you had to be sneaky, but nowadays, you can slide into someone's email inbox or social media direct messages without anyone being the wiser. With all the technology we have, sin is even easier to slip into. Take care not to worship from your faulty wires. It doesn't matter how "saved" you are; seduction feels good, especially if you're hungry for praise, respect, and intimacy.

Proverbs 7:21 says, "With much seductive speech she persuades him; with her smooth talk she compels him." A man desires for his ego to be stroked. When his ego isn't being stroked, he tends to go somewhere it can be stroked, even if that means turning to a woman who is less desirable than his wife.

Men, we need to be disciplined, and we need to be careful. Even though I've talked about certain things our wives can do to help us, it's up to us men to know what is right and do what is right. If we fail in that, it's no one's fault but our own.

If you've made some mistakes, you need to ask God for forgiveness and get back on track. As leaders in our homes and in our families, we need to take responsibility for actions and set godly examples. Why throw away your marriage, your family, and your integrity over momentary pleasures? We need to recognize when we are operating out of our faulty wiring and choose instead to follow God.

Proverbs 7:24–27 says of the adulterous woman:

And now, O sons, listen to me, and be attentive to the words of my mouth. Let not your heart turn aside to her ways; do not stray into her paths, for many a victim has she laid low, and all her slain are a mighty throng. Her house is the way to Sheol, going down to the chambers of death.

Many a strong and anointed man has been pulled down by seduction. Be careful and guard your heart. We cannot allow ourselves to place anything higher than God in our lives. If we are close to God, He will warn us when we start to stray, and He will help us to get back on the right path. But all too often, we don't have time for God, and we end up functioning from our faulty wires.

WORSHIP FROM GOD'S LOVE

So, what does rightly wired worship look like? It focuses on God's love above any other thing. Wrongly wired worship comes from our flesh, but rightly wired worship is all about the love of God. Do you remember the story of Joseph and Potiphar's wife in Genesis 39? She repeatedly tried to get Joseph to sleep with her, but he told her, "Behold, because of me my master has no concern about anything in the house, and he has put everything that he has in my charge. He is not greater in this house than I am, nor has he kept back anything from me except you, because you are his wife. How then can I do this great wickedness and sin against God?" (Genesis 39:8–9).

This was before God gave us His law. There was no commandment at that point that said you couldn't have another man's wife, but there was something inside Joseph that led him to say, "I can't do this against my God." That's what we need to be able to say to ourselves when we start to feel that pull toward our faulty wiring.

We are to love God so much that our flesh has to die. God

loves us too much and has been too good to us for us to choose to go out like that. He has delivered us and shown us too much grace for us to go back to our old, sinful ways. We need to choose not to go back to our faulty wiring—not because we don't have it in us, but because we love God too much. When we focus on God's love and on worshiping Him, there are certain things that we just won't feel comfortable doing.

First John 4:7–8 says, "Beloved, let us love one another, for love is from God, and whoever loves has been born of God and knows God. Anyone who does not love does not know God, because God is love." If you look at the Ten Commandments, they are all based in love. You won't steal from someone you love. You won't kill someone you love or sleep with that person's spouse. You won't dishonor your parents if you love them. You won't have any other gods before God if you love Him.

If we focus on God loving us and on us loving God, there's a whole lot of stuff we won't get into. If we worship from a heart of love for God, there are things we just won't fall for. You might have fallen for those things in the past, but you aren't going to stay there forever. You're going to get up and keep going. The devil can no longer deceive you in those areas, because God's love has been so lavishly good to you. Recognizing that, now that's winning!

This is why when we are seeking love, we first need to think about the greatest love of all: God's love. First Corinthians 13:4–8 tells us:

Love is patient and kind; love does not envy or boast; it is not arrogant or rude. It does not insist on its own way; it is not irritable or resentful; it does not rejoice at wrongdoing, but rejoices with the truth. Love bears all things, believes all things, hopes all things, endures all things. Love never ends.

Human love and human relationships will fail you, but the love of God will never fail you. He will always be there for you, and that's why you should never put anything above God. There is no one in your life who has been as consistent as God. He is there when you sit down and when you rise up, and He knows everything about you. He knows the number of hairs on your head, and He knows you by name. If anyone deserves your love, it's God.

If you focus on God and His love for you, His love will cleanse you, deliver you, and help you to walk in victory (Romans 8:35–39). You won't be worshiping out of faulty wiring. You'll be walking in the love of God. You'll be walking in victory through the Spirit, not the flesh.

THE RELATIONSHIP BETWEEN WEALTH AND WORSHIP

Besides human relationships, other types of things can also interfere with properly wired worship by replacing God as our focus. One of the major stumbling blocks to a correctly wired worship is wealth, or material things. Many people fall into the trap of worshiping wealth instead of giving God wealthy worship.

People will commit any number of sins for money. Some people steal money, and they will certainly lie for it. They may kill one another for it, too. How often in history has wealth motivated nations to invade and ravage one another? All of this testifies to the fact that too many people regard money with the kind of intense respect and devotion they ought to give only to God. If the church would worship God the way the rest of the world worships money, imagine what kind of world we might find ourselves living in!

In thinking about the relationship between wealth and worship, I want to frame it in terms of these three foundational questions:

- Is your worship rich?

- Do you worship your wealth?

- Do you worship with your wealth?

Being rich goes beyond having an abundance of material wealth. *Rich* can also mean "having high value or quality," being "magnificently impressive," being "vivid and deep in color," being "highly productive," or "being pure or nearly pure."[12]

Is your worship rich? Is it of high value and quality? Is it impressive and deep? Is it productive? Is it pure? Do you approach worship full of energy and excitement, hardly able to wait for the opportunity to praise God? If the answer is consistently no, your worship isn't truly rich.

Rich worship doesn't happen only at church. You ought

to worship at your house and in your car, at work and running errands. Once, at home, my wife and I were watching a movie when our young daughter got a blueberry stuck in her throat and couldn't breathe. My wife reacted quickly, performing the Heimlich to dislodge it. By God's grace, our daughter lived. When we went back to watching the movie, God asked me why I wasn't worshiping Him for sparing our daughter's life. Of course, I had thanked God and was grateful, but the way I nonchalantly went back to the movie showed a level of imbalance in my worship.

Too often, when something bad happens, we're quick to cry out to God, "Why?" or "Help me!" But when we're spared, we take it for granted, failing to magnify Him the way we magnify our distress in times of trouble. We fail to praise and glorify God deeply and abundantly. Our worship needs to be richer! If we were to stop and thank God for every specific thing He does for us, we would never have time to do anything other than give Him thanks. Doing things throughout the day shouldn't stop us from worshiping Him richly and continuously in some way. That means our lives as a whole must be rich toward God.

Ephesians 2:4 begins, "But God, being rich in mercy...." Those first two words—"But God"—say so much! When we are at our lowest and weakest, He saves us by the richness of His mercy and grace. He demonstrates His goodness to us in this life, and He has even more abundant goodness to show us after this life. If eternity were up to me, I know I'd mess it up, but God took it out of my hands and put it in the blood of Jesus Christ. That's how I'm saved, by His amazing grace, not by my worship or anything else I do. If God is so rich in His mercy and grace toward us, why wouldn't we want to be rich in our worship of Him? His grace is extravagant and abundant, and our worship should be the same. Whether we're in church or mowing the lawn, our lives should abundantly show gratitude to God.

WORSHIPING WEALTH

Do not lay up for yourselves treasures on earth, where moth and rust destroy and where thieves break in and steal, but lay up for yourselves treasures in heaven, where neither moth nor rust destroys and where thieves do not break in and steal. For where your treasure is, there your heart will be also.

—Matthew 6:19–21

You can't worship God richly if you're worshiping someone or something else instead. That goes for relationships with other people, as we've previously discussed, and it goes for money and the things money can buy. It applies to any cause, goal, or object of our desire other than God Himself.

Jesus pointed out that the things this world offers do not last; they fade and deteriorate. Even homes that appreciate in value can deteriorate or be destroyed. No matter how big and fancy a house is, it could burn down in mere minutes. Your health won't last forever, either. No matter how young and healthy you are, you're in the process of dying. You're a dust bunny destined to return to the dust of the earth, and so am I. Given this reality, we had better put our hope in eternal things and give our praise and worship to our eternal God!

Material treasures and other things of this world may be good and proper in their place. Working to earn money has its place. Even so, temporary treasures should not drive us; they cannot be our focus. Trendy clothes, new cars, and physical beauty all lose their luster sooner or later. You can have some of these things as long as you're not worshiping them as your true treasure. Our truest treasure is whatever dominates our thoughts and decisions. Where your treasure lies, that's where your heart is, and your heart should belong to God.

No one can serve two masters, for either he will hate the one and love the other, or he will be devoted to the one and despise the other. You cannot serve God and money.
—Matthew 6:24

Money will try to master you. The world wants you to serve money, not God, and don't kid yourself: you cannot truly serve both. You cannot serve God *and* something else. If you're confident that God is the sole focus of your worship, ask yourself:

- If you get a bad report or a good report about finances, how does it affect your worship?

- If you didn't have the financial means you currently have, how would that affect your worship?

- If God were to ask you to be generous in a way you haven't before, how would that affect your worship?

Some of us may find that our honest answers to these questions give us pause, revealing where the real treasure of our hearts is. Remember that Jesus told us to "seek first the kingdom of God and his righteousness" (Matthew 6:33). Our focus and priorities ought to be on the Kingdom at all times—at the beginning and end of every day and in between as well, even while we are tending to the natural things, our responsibilities in the world. A Kingdom focus will produce worship in our hearts throughout the day!

WORSHIPING WITH YOUR WEALTH

When you are wired for wealthy worship of God, your heart will be focused on Him, and you will direct your resources accordingly. That's what I call worshiping with your wealth. If a person is seeking first the Kingdom in his or her heart, no one will be able to stop that person from giving. Givers give because that is what they do.

Now, I am not going to chastise those who are not in the habit of being generous. I'm just going to encourage you to look to those who are worshiping God with their generosity.

Then reflect on where your heart is and where your treasure lies. Which seems to be resulting in the more victorious life, generosity or poor stewardship?

Stewardship, all the ways you handle your money, is worship. Glorify God by being fruitful and multiplying (Genesis 1:28) in the handling of your resources. The question of stewardship is this: How do I function with or handle all the resources at my disposal? The answer to this question shows whom you serve.

> One who is faithful in a very little is also faithful in much, and one who is dishonest in a very little is also dishonest in much. If then you have not been faithful in the unrighteous wealth, who will entrust to you the true riches? And if you have not been faithful in that which is another's, who will give you that which is your own? No servant can serve two masters....
> **—Luke 16:10–13**

In other words, if you won't do right with a few dollars, you can't be trusted with millions. God tests you with a little, and you won't graduate without passing the test. In the kingdom of God, money is the lowest level of riches, so the money test is the most basic test of stewardship.

The concept of stewardship boils down to this: it's God's money, His food, His clothes, His house—His stuff. Yes, God sometimes provides you with material things, but He does not only give stuff *to* you; He also gives stuff *through* you. If someone were to give you a whole dish of your favorite food, would you overcome your instinct to hoard it for yourself and instead share it with people you love? Like other things of this world, the food won't last forever, anyway. Why not share it so everyone can be blessed? Similarly, money is like a whole pie. Certainly, you're going to eat some of the pieces yourself, but what do you do with the rest? How you handle the rest shows either greed or generosity.

Money will try to become your master, but it's supposed to be your servant. That's almost like children who try to tell their parents what to do when it's supposed to be the other way around. My wife and I don't let our three children dictate our major life decisions, and you can't let attachment to wealth control your decision-making, either. Don't let money be the boss. Keep it in its place.

Through good stewardship—that is, worshiping God with your wealth—money will serve you. You worship God when you sow some of your wealth into His church, such as by tithing or offerings. You can also worship Him by saving money, like Joseph did when Pharaoh set him over management of Egypt's food resources (Genesis 41). Joseph wisely and discerningly responded to God's direction and Pharaoh's trust by saving resources during abundant times to prepare for lean times.

Sometimes wise stewardship requires you to "cast your bread upon the waters" (Ecclesiastes 11:1), investing and putting money in places where it will return to you later. Don't be afraid to ask God to lead you regarding how to invest in different places, "for you do not know which will prosper" (Ecclesiastes 11:6). It's also not wrong to spend money on your own needs and desires, because God "richly provides us with everything to enjoy" (1 Timothy 6:17). This is all part of winning through wealthy, properly wired worship.

Just keep in mind that you cannot buy happiness with your money. Money is only an answer to all things (Ecclesiastes 10:19) that are properly matters of money. Material wealth is something, but it is far from everything. Use it to worship the one who *is* everything: God.

NOTHING CAN GET BETWEEN US AND GOD'S LOVE

There's one truth I'd like to leave you with, the truth about deliverance. In this chapter, we've discussed many things that can cause our hearts to be misaligned in their focus and mess up our wiring for worship. Prolonged misalignment can result in forms of addiction. Often addictions slip into our lives and grab hold of us when we are not properly worshiping God, and we end up worshiping those addictions. We tell ourselves, "I'm not going to give in to that addiction today. I'm not going to do what it wants me to do," and that addiction will say, "Oh yes, you are!"

That's why in my church congregation, Deliverance Temple, our goal is to confess our deliverance consistently. We refuse to let anything keep us down. We refuse to lose. Our focus is not on the mistakes of the past, but on the possibilities of the future.

Come hell or high water, we will worship the God who

can deliver us. If He doesn't deliver us today, He will deliver us tomorrow. If He doesn't deliver us tomorrow, He will deliver us a year from now, ten years from now, or on our dying day. Whatever the timing, we know that we will be delivered, we will win, and we will be who God says we can be.

We worship God and proclaim Him as a deliverer to others even when we have yet to be completely delivered ourselves. Deliverance is a process. We worship God based on where we're headed, not just where we are or where we've come from.

Paul said it best in Romans 8:38–39: "For I am sure that neither death nor life, nor angels nor rulers, nor things present nor things to come, nor powers, nor height nor depth, nor anything else in all creation, will be able to separate us from the love of God in Christ Jesus our Lord."

If we can get back to worshiping, first and foremost, from our love relationship with God, the church will truly be the church. Revival and the deliverance that comes from it will break out across the land. We've been waiting on God for these things, but He is waiting on us.

May God help us to tear down any idols that we have put above Him—whether it's human relationships, material wealth, career, entertainment, hobbies, or habits—and give us the strength and humility to repent and ask His forgiveness. May we turn away from worshiping from the faulty wiring of our flesh and begin to worship from His love and walk in victory in the Spirit.

Chapter Two Questions

Question: What things do you have the tendency to put above God? What changes can you make to ensure that God remains first in your life?

_____

_____

_____

_____

_____

_____

_____

_____

_____

_____

_____

_____

Question: In what ways does your worship of God reveal the wiring of your fallen nature? In what areas do you need God to rewire your heart so you can worship Him the way He intended when He created you?

_____

_____

_____

_____

_____

_____

_____

_____

_____

_____

Question: Are there any indications that you are putting God on the back burner in your life? What are those indications and what changes can you make to bring God to the forefront?

_____

_____

_____

_____

_____

_____

_____

_____

_____

_____

_____

Question: In what ways are you putting human relationships above God?

_____

_____

_____

_____

_____

_____

_____

_____

_____

_____

_____

Question: Is money more important to you than God? Is your worship rich? Is it of high value and quality? Is it impressive and deep? Is it pure? Is it productive?

_____

_____

_____

_____

_____

_____

_____

_____

_____

_____

_____

Question: What addictions are evident in your life? How can worship be a part of helping to deliver you from those addictions?

_____

_____

_____

_____

_____

_____

_____

_____

_____

_____

_____

Action: In a notebook or journal, make a list of your actions, behaviors, and thoughts throughout the day. Next to each one, write whether or not it was motivated by love. How much of what you do, think, and say is motivated by your love for God?

Chapter Two Notes

_____

_____

_____

_____

_____

_____

_____

_____

_____

_____

_____

_____

_____

_____

_____

CHAPTER THREE

Wise Worship

Proverbs 4:7 tells us, "The beginning of wisdom is this: Get wisdom, and whatever you get, get insight." Wisdom is a foundational principle, and it is essential to our lives. We need to grab it, absorb it, and use it.

Jesus further illustrated the importance of wisdom in Matthew 7:24–27:

> *Everyone then who hears these words of mine and does them will be like a wise man who built his house on the rock. And the rain fell, and the floods came, and the winds blew and beat on that house, but it did not fall, because it had been founded on the rock. And everyone who hears these words of mine and does not do them will be like a foolish man who built his house on the sand. And the rain fell, and the floods came, and the winds blew and beat against that house, and it fell, and great was the fall of it.*

We should build our lives on a foundation of wisdom, and that applies to our worship as well: we need to exercise wise worship, worship that is based in wisdom. Wise worship is also *worthy* and *wired* because it's based on a correct understanding of who God is and of our relationship with Him. Scripture provides excellent examples of what constitutes foolish worship and what constitutes wise worship in the stories of King Uzziah of Judah and the prophet Isaiah, respectively.

UZZIAH BEGAN WITH WISDOM

Uzziah started well, living a life marked by wisdom, but his end was tragic and marked by pride. We are introduced to Uzziah in 2 Chronicles 26:1: "And all the people of Judah took Uzziah, who was sixteen years old, and made him king instead of his father Amaziah." Age alone does not determine wisdom. You can be wise as a young person, and you can be wise as an old person. Society tends to think that people become wiser as they grow older, but our wisdom does not depend solely on our age. We've all met older people who are foolish.

Let's jump ahead to 2 Chronicles 26:4: "And he did what was right in the eyes of the LORD, according to all that his father Amaziah had done." It takes wisdom to know when to follow your ancestors and when not to follow them. You shouldn't do everything your father did unless everything he did is right for you and your life. You shouldn't follow the path your ancestors followed if it isn't the path God has given you.

For example, if you take over the family business when

that isn't what God has asked you to do, you could end up destroying the business. You need to have the wisdom to discern the path that God has for you. Sometimes you shouldn't do anything your ancestors did because everything they did was wrong, and you need to have the wisdom to know how to move in a different direction.

Second Chronicles 26:5 continues, "He set himself to seek God in the days of Zechariah, who instructed him in the fear of God, and as long as he sought the LORD, God made him prosper." Wisdom requires a posture of continually seeking God. We're never so wise that we no longer need to pursue Him! I'm a pastor, but I often tell God that I don't know what I'm doing without His guidance.

That's why you have to go beyond Sunday morning service and get to a place where you are seeking God earnestly and diligently, even radically. That's a lifestyle of worship. In this day and age, we need God's wisdom more than ever before if we are to see victory in our lives.

Uzziah also had the blessing of a spiritual father, Zechariah. Zechariah was a leader who taught Uzziah to do what was right in the eyes of the Lord. Following his example, Uzziah humbled himself and sought the Lord and the wisdom of those who came before him. We will never be so wise on our own that we no longer have a need for the godly leadership and wisdom of others.

Uzziah's wisdom here reminds us of what we learned about wealth in the last chapter: wisdom knows that true prosperity comes from seeking God. In Matthew 6:33, Jesus said, "But seek first the kingdom of God and his righteousness, and all these things will be added to you." We can obtain prosperity outside of seeking God, but it's not true prosperity, and it will lead us down rabbit holes that we can't get out of. Some people have sold themselves to the devil without even realizing it, because they've pursued prosperity in the wrong way. As Christians, we don't want any wealth that comes to us apart from God.

Second Chronicles 26:6–7 says of Uzziah, "He went out and made war against the Philistines and broke through the wall of Gath and the wall of Jabneh and the wall of Ashdod, and he built cities in the territory of Ashdod and elsewhere among the Philistines. God helped him against the Philistines and against the Arabians who lived in Gurbaal and against the Meunites."

Wisdom is proactive against the enemy, not just reactive. We need to be stepping on the devil's territory before he has an opportunity to steal from us or attack us. We need to be proactive and pick a fight with the devil before he even shows up. How do we pick a fight with the devil? We do it through our worship, a worship that incorporates pleading the victorious blood of Jesus over ourselves, our lives, and everyone and everything connected to us. We don't sit there, waiting for the devil to show up and mess us around. We rebuke him in Christ's name in advance so that he won't even think about setting foot near us.

Wisdom also knows that God's help is needed for victory in every battle and against every enemy. There will never be a time in your life when you will not need God. If His presence doesn't go into battle with us, we may as well not even bother, because there's no way we're going to win without Him.

UZZIAH WAS FINISHED BY PRIDE

Second Chronicles 26:8 continues, "The Ammonites paid tribute to Uzziah, and his fame spread even to the border of Egypt, for he became very strong." That's another characteristic of wisdom: it knows how to handle fame. There's nothing wrong with having fame, but you need to know how to handle it properly. Handling fame properly means that fame must always be a backseat passenger and never a front-seat driver.

When you receive accolades and recognition, you must not allow them to become the driving force behind your life. At the end of the day, it doesn't matter how famous or successful you are, who knows your name, or who's asking for your autograph. You're still human, and you shouldn't forget where you came from. Always ask yourself why you're doing what you're doing and make sure that your motives honor God. Humble yourself before the Lord. Don't let fame, recognition, or success go to your head.

If we refuse to humble ourselves, we will find ourselves becoming proud, and wisdom cannot coexist with pride. That's exactly what happened to Uzziah in 2 Chronicles 26:16: "But when he was strong, he grew proud, to his destruction. For he was unfaithful to the LORD his God and entered the temple of the LORD to burn incense on the altar of incense."

Uzziah had been doing so well up to this point. Of all the kings of the Northern and Southern Kingdoms, there were only eight whom God said were good kings, and Uzziah was one of them.[13] Pride is the original sin, and if the devil is going to try to tempt us with anything, he's going to try to tempt us with what he knows best: pride. Satan himself was an anointed cherub until he succumbed to pride (Ezekiel 28:11–19).

If you are functioning from pride, you are unwise. You are headed toward foolishness and will soon be functioning in folly. When we look at ourselves, we really don't have anything to be proud of. We came from dust, and to dust we shall return. It is only God's hand that sustains us. We are frail and finite, and we need God in everything. He is the one who takes care of us and protects us from dangers seen and unseen. He has been faithful to us, so we should not be unwise and get caught up in pride.

Second Chronicles 26:17–18 continues, "But Azariah the priest went in after him, with eighty priests of the LORD who were men of valor, and they withstood King Uzziah and said to him, 'It is not for you, Uzziah, to burn incense to the LORD, but for the priests, the sons of Aaron, who are consecrated to burn incense. Go out of the sanctuary, for you have done wrong, and it will bring you no honor from the LORD God.'"

Unwise worship has unintended consequences. Because Uzziah was being blessed and doing so well, he went into the temple and started doing things that were supposed to be done by the priests. The priests confronted him, but Uzziah felt that he had the right to do these things because he was the king. He needed to stay in his spiritual lane.

If you don't have the grace or the anointing for something, don't get into that lane. If God has made it clear to you that He doesn't want you to preach, for example, then you shouldn't try to preach—whether it's from a pulpit, on a street corner, or on social media. Don't get caught up in what you think you should be doing. Rather, humbly seek God and do only what He wants you to do.

Uzziah was wise initially, but he tried to take his pride into his worship, and it ruined everything. He was worshiping God, but he was out of order in how he was doing it. The consequences for Uzziah were instantaneous:

Then Uzziah was angry. Now he had a censer in his hand to burn incense, and when he became angry with the priests, leprosy broke out on his forehead in the presence of the priests in the house of the LORD, by the altar of incense. And Azariah the chief priest and all the priests looked at him, and behold, he was leprous in his forehead! And they rushed him out quickly, and he himself hurried to go out, because the LORD had struck him. And King Uzziah was a leper to the day of his death, and being a leper lived in a separate house, for he was excluded from the house of the LORD. And Jotham his son was over the king's household, governing the people of the land.
—2 Chronicles 26:19–21

In many cases, by the time we realize that we have succumbed to pride, it's too late; consequences have already been set in motion. Uzziah was in a hurry to leave the temple because he knew that he had crossed a line, but by that time, he was already leprous. He was already experiencing the consequences of his pride. Uzziah started out well, but he finished horribly.

Don't allow your life to be characterized by your mistakes. If you start well, continue strong, and aim to finish well. God will give you space to fix the mistakes you make. If your heart is proud, however, you likely will not acknowledge your mistakes, and you won't be able to fix them with God's grace, either.

Wise worship knows that God uses us, but He doesn't need any one person in particular. You need God, but He doesn't need you. God will use you, but He doesn't need you. He wants you, but He doesn't need you. We need to have the wisdom to thank Him for using us. Humble yourself under the mighty hand of God and thank Him for choosing to use you.

ISAIAH EXEMPLIFIED WISE
AND HUMBLE WORSHIP

We've learned through the life of Uzziah that pride is foolish worship. What, then, is wise worship? Uzziah's cousin Isaiah, a prophet, taught us that humility is wise worship and gave us an example to follow.[14][15] Isaiah said, "In the year that King Uzziah died I saw the Lord sitting upon a throne, high and lifted up; and the train of his robe filled the temple" (Isaiah 6:1). Wise worship sees God even in bad situations.

Isaiah's vision of God occurred in the same year that Uzziah died a tragic death because of his pride.

Now, it is not my desire for anyone to be prideful, but you can certainly learn a lot from watching someone who is operating from a proud heart. You can witness someone else's mistake and decide that you're going to do something different. I believe that Isaiah learned from Uzziah's tragic end.

Wise people will learn from others' mistakes and not have to make those mistakes themselves. There are some things that we have no business dabbling in, because we've seen what's happened to family members or other people in our lives who have done those things.

Isaiah 6:2–3, 5 continues:

Above him stood the seraphim. Each had six wings: with two he covered his face, and with two he covered his feet, and with two he flew. And one called to another and said: "Holy, holy, holy is the LORD of hosts; the whole earth is full of his glory!" ... And I said: "Woe is me! For I am lost; for I am a man of unclean lips, and I dwell in the midst of a people of unclean lips; for my eyes have seen the King, the LORD of hosts!"

Wise worship recognizes God for His holiness and His glory. This is the opposite of the pride that Uzziah demonstrated and the epitome of humility, as Isaiah demonstrated. When Isaiah saw the Lord, he acknowledged that he was a mess. He knew that he had no business being prideful and elevating himself to God's level. Isaiah recognized that God was holy and that he was not, unless he was connected to God. It should be clear to us, as it was to Isaiah, that we are nothing without God.

Isaiah 6:6–7 describes God's solution for Isaiah's lack of holiness: "Then one of the seraphim flew to me, having in his hand a burning coal that he had taken with tongs from the altar. And he touched my mouth and said: 'Behold, this has touched your lips; your guilt is taken away, and your sin atoned for.'"

Wise worship trusts God to handle our flesh, our iniquity, and our sin. When Isaiah recognized how sinful he was in comparison to the holiness of God, God didn't ask him to fix it. The angel came and purged Isaiah of his sin by touching a coal from God's altar to Isaiah's lips. Likewise, even though we may sin, we are no longer absolutely sinful, because the blood of the Lamb has touched our lives. Although we sin, we are no longer considered sinners, because God's grace meets us at the point of our need. You are no longer a liar, an adulterer, a gossiper, or another type of sinner, because God has touched your life and made you whole. We are purged by grace, like Isaiah was purged by the burning coal.

One of the worst things you can do is try to fix your own sin. Whether you try to hide it, cover it up, or overcome it through sheer willpower, all you'll do is wear yourself out. Instead of trying to fix your own sin, you need to ask God to cleanse you. You need to agree to do things His way. You need to allow His grace to do the work and enable you to win.

God is not as worried about our sin as we are. We tend to want it fixed overnight, but He takes His time because when

He does it, He does it right. There are things in your life that aren't right yet, but God isn't in a rush to fix them, because He is fixing you in such a way that it will humble you. That way, once you are delivered, you won't be proud and start pointing your finger at the things that need to be fixed in other people's lives. You can simply rejoice that God has delivered you, give Him the glory for it, and pray for others to know the same grace that God has given you. You can trust God to take care of everything in your life.

Isaiah 6:8 continues, "And I heard the voice of the Lord saying, 'Whom shall I send, and who will go for us?' Then I said, 'Here I am! Send me.'" God is more concerned with our availability than our ability. God appreciates it when we make ourselves available for His purpose for our lives. A posture of availability signals to God that we want to be used by Him.

When you ask God to use you, He will use you, but He may not use you in the way you want. Even so, you are far better off being with God and experiencing the troubles that come with God's assignment for your life than being with the devil and experiencing the troubles that come with the devil's plan for you. The devil cannot be trusted, so I've chosen to follow God's plan for my life. And let me tell you this: the Lord has never let me down, not even once. He *always* wins, and since I am in Him, so do I.

WICKED WORSHIP

God's grace can overcome our weakness. However, I believe that there's a stark difference between weakness and wickedness. We can be moving in a good, wise, and correct direction and still be moved off the path that we should be on if we yield to wickedness. Paul summed it up best in Galatians 5:7: "You were running well. Who hindered you from obeying the truth?" You can be following a lifestyle of worthy and wise worship that honors God, but then something hinders you and you end up in wicked worship. We absolutely do not want to end up in wicked worship.

Uzziah did very well until pride was found in him, and then he had a tragic fall. He moved from wise worship into wicked worship. It's important that we listen to the Holy Spirit to determine whether we have shifted into wicked worship and, if so, in what ways.

The quintessential sign that you have a lifestyle of wise and worthy worship is God's presence with you. In Exodus 33:15–16, Moses said to God, "If your presence will not go with me, do not bring us up from here. For how shall it be known that I have found favor in your sight, I and your people? Is it not in your going with us, so that we are distinct, I and your people, from every other people on the face of the earth?"

It's not just about getting into God's presence when you're worshiping at church. It's about God's presence actually being with you all the time. His presence isn't confined to a Sunday or midweek service. If you are truly living a life of worship, His presence will still be with you when you leave the church building. Like Moses, you won't go anywhere unless God's presence is with you.

I like how the Good News Translation renders Exodus

33:16: "How will anyone know that you are pleased with your people and with me if you do not go with us? Your presence with us will distinguish us from any other people on earth" (GNT). God loves everyone, but the people who carry His presence are supposed to be set apart from everyone else. There should be something about the people who have the presence of God that makes them different from those who do not.

The something that should make us different is explained in Galatians 6:9–10: "And let us not grow weary of doing good, for in due season we will reap, if we do not give up. So then, as we have opportunity, let us do good to everyone, and especially to those who are of the household of faith." We are to do good to everyone, but we are to be especially good to those who are fellow believers.

WICKED DISTINCTIONS ARE WICKED WORSHIP

Scripture makes it clear that we are to be distinguished by God's presence above all else. I'm concerned that instead of focusing on what distinguishes us, too many Christians have given way to distinctions. For example, there are people in the church who claim that as long as you believe in Jesus, you're their brother or sister in Christ, but if they find out that you voted differently from them, they want nothing to do with you. Other distinctions that believers make include how a person was baptized, what denomination someone belongs to, and even what Bible translation a person reads. Some believers go beyond this pettiness and make distinctions based on a person's race, gender, or socio-economic status.

> My brothers, show no partiality as you hold the faith in our Lord Jesus Christ, the Lord of glory. For if a man wearing a gold ring and fine clothing comes into your assembly, and a poor man in shabby clothing also comes in, and if you pay attention to the one who wears the fine clothing and say, "You sit here in a good place," while you say to the poor man, "You stand over there," or, "Sit down at my feet," have you not then made distinctions among yourselves and become judges with evil thoughts?
>
> **—James 2:1–4**

Make no mistake: God is disgusted by such things because it means that His people have shifted into wicked worship. We are supposed to be focusing on the fact that we are distinguished by God's presence with us, but instead there has been too much focus on the distinctions between us.

God set apart a people for Himself, that they would go into the world, reach other people, and bring them to Him. But the people who are set apart for God have been fighting among themselves. Historically, we let racism and gender differences get in the way, and we twisted Scripture to justify and support these behaviors. We allowed distinctions to come in front of what should have distinguished us, which is God's Spirit dwelling in each of us.

We have a way of allowing the things that should bring us together to take a backseat to all the little things that keep us apart. If we are part of the family of God, we should be able to come together. Galatians 3:26 reminds us that "in Christ

Jesus you are all sons of God, through faith." We are part of God's family not because of anything we have done, but through faith. We are saved by grace through faith, and there's something about faith that ought to connect us with each other.

All of us have the same blood—not O negative or B positive, but the blood of Jesus Christ, the Righteous One. If you have the blood of the Lamb, we are family. We are connected.

Galatians 3:27–28 states, "For as many of you as were baptized into Christ have put on Christ. There is neither Jew nor Greek, there is neither slave nor free, there is no male and female, for you are all one in Christ Jesus." Because we have been baptized into Christ, there are no distinctions. There is no black or white. There is no rich or poor. There is no Republican or Democrat. There is nothing that supersedes who we are in Christ. We are all part of God's family. We need to double down on this and do it better than we've ever done before, because there is a wicked spirit in this age that's trying to tear believers apart from each other with all these other distinctions.

This doesn't mean that we will always agree on everything. Sometimes distinctions come on the heels of disagreements, and disagreements happen because we are all human. Sometimes we have to agree to disagree (Acts 15). For example, I may never vote the way you vote, but if you're saved, we still have something in common. We should still be able to communicate and function together without taking things out on one another or hindering the work of God.

LOVE IS THE CURE FOR WICKED WORSHIP

How, then, do we accomplish this? How do we overcome distinctions and do good to others, especially our fellow believers, with whom we may disagree? First John 4:7–8, 11 has the answer:

> *Beloved, let us love one another, for love is from God, and whoever loves has been born of God and knows God. Anyone who does not love does not know God, because God is love. ... Beloved, if God so loved us, we also ought to love one another.*

It's about love, not about skin color, gender, or any other distinction. Don't withhold your love from someone based on a distinction. God shouldn't even like us, yet He loves us in spite of ourselves. Who are we, then, to dislike other people because of their distinctions? We need to put our hands over our mouths before we say ignorant things and dishonor God's creation. If God paid the price for other people's sins as well as ours, then we need to learn to love everybody.

This is illustrated perfectly in the Parable of the Unforgiving Servant in Matthew 18:21–35:

> *Then Peter came up and said to him, "Lord, how often will my brother sin against me, and I forgive him? As many as seven times?" Jesus said to him, "I do not say to you seven times, but seventy-seven times.*

"Therefore the kingdom of heaven may be compared to a king who wished to settle accounts with his servants. When he began to settle, one was brought to him who owed him ten thousand talents. And since he could not pay, his master ordered him to be sold, with his wife and children and all that he had, and payment to be made. So the servant fell on his knees, imploring him, 'Have patience with me, and I will pay you everything.' And out of pity for him, the master of that servant released him and forgave him the debt. But when that same servant went out, he found one of his fellow servants who owed him a hundred denarii, and seizing him, he began to choke him, saying, 'Pay what you owe.' So his fellow servant fell down and pleaded with him, 'Have patience with me, and I will pay you.' He refused and went and put him in prison until he should pay the debt. When his fellow servants saw what had taken place, they were greatly distressed, and they went and reported to their master all that had taken place. Then his master summoned him and said to him, 'You wicked servant! I forgave you all that debt because you pleaded with me. And should not you have had mercy on your fellow servant, as I had mercy on you?' And in anger his master delivered him to the jailers, until he should pay all his debt. So also my heavenly Father will do to every one of you, if you do not forgive your brother from your heart."

God has forgiven you over and over again. If, in spite of that, you can't bring yourself to get along with other people because of the color of their skin or their gender, that is wicked worship. It's twisted, and it makes no sense in light of God's grace toward you.

MAKE YOUR WORSHIP WORTHY AGAIN

In order for us to shift from wicked worship back to worthy worship, we need to refrain from putting our distinctions before that which distinguishes us as God's people—namely, His presence. The godly people have to stand up, and the righteous have to rise up. We can't afford to sit on the sidelines while this focus on distinctions—on race, on gender, on denominations, on political affiliations—tears apart the household of God, our communities, and our world. Stand up for people who are being treated wrongly, whether it's inside or outside the church.

> *He has told you, O man, what is good; and what does the LORD require of you but to do justice, and to love kindness, and to walk humbly with your God?*
>
> *—Micah 6:8*

We need to switch from wicked worship to wise, properly wired, worthy worship, and we accomplish this by learning to love our neighbor. Who is our neighbor? Jesus answered this question in the Parable of the Good Samaritan. To provide some context, the Samaritans were a people of mixed race who were looked down upon and regarded as inferior by the godly Israelites.[16][17] Let's look at Luke 10:29–37:

> *But he [the lawyer], desiring to justify himself, said to Jesus, "And who is my neighbor?" Jesus replied, "A man was going down from Jerusalem to Jericho, and he fell among robbers,*

who stripped him and beat him and departed, leaving him half dead. Now by chance a priest was going down that road, and when he saw him he passed by on the other side. So likewise a Levite, when he came to the place and saw him, passed by on the other side. But a Samaritan, as he journeyed, came to where he was, and when he saw him, he had compassion. He went to him and bound up his wounds, pouring on oil and wine. Then he set him on his own animal and brought him to an inn and took care of him. And the next day he took out two denarii and gave them to the innkeeper, saying, 'Take care of him, and whatever more you spend, I will repay you when I come back.' Which of these three, do you think, proved to be a neighbor to the man who fell among the robbers?" He said, "The one who showed him mercy." And Jesus said to him, "You go, and do likewise."

This is how we should be if we want to get out of wicked worship. Have you, like the priest and the Levite, been so busy coming to church that you haven't taken time to be the church? If you've been raised so high that you can't stoop down to help someone else, you have a wicked worship. If, on the other hand, your heart breaks for humanity, regardless of race and other distinctions, then God will most certainly use you.

May God make us one and help us to love on all of humanity. Do not hold hate in your heart toward anyone, because you run the risk of living a wicked life and offering a wicked worship to God. Be like the Samaritan, not the unforgiving servant. Examine your heart for pride and ask God to keep you humble so that you may be like Isaiah, not Uzziah. With God's help, our worship can be worthy, properly wired, wise, and honoring to God.

Chapter Three Questions

Question: Is seeking God and His wisdom a continual part of your life? What shifts do you need to make in order for turning to God to be your default reaction?

_____

_____

_____

_____

_____

_____

_____

_____

_____

_____

_____

Question: Describe any areas of your life where pride is attempting to rear its head. How can you pursue humility in those areas?

_____

_____

_____

_____

_____

_____

_____

_____

_____

_____

Question: Is trusting God to cleanse you of your sin currently a part of your worship? What sins do you need to confess and allow God's grace to remove from you?

_____

_____

_____

_____

_____

_____

_____

_____

_____

_____

Question: Are there any areas where you veer into distinction and division regarding other believers in Christ? Do you think that those divisions are in alignment with a lifestyle of worship? Why or why not?

_____

_____

_____

_____

_____

_____

_____

_____

_____

_____

_____

Action: If there is anyone in your life with whom a distinction has become a disagreement to the point of a severed relationship, spend some time in prayer, asking God if reconciliation with that person is possible. If it is, ask God to show you the steps you can take to begin pursuing that reconciliation.

Chapter Three Notes

Winning Worship

The word *win* means to "be successful or victorious in (a contest or conflict)."[18] We tend to understand about contests, but we sometimes forget about conflicts. Living as we do in a fallen and sinful world, we are in constant conflict because of our faith in Christ. Our conflicts are by faith, and we need to learn how to live and worship victoriously in these conflicts.

In 1 Corinthians 9:23, Paul stated, "I do it all for the sake of the gospel, that I may share with them in its blessings." When we talk about winning, we aren't just talking about going to heaven. That is the ultimate win and the ultimate goal, but there are some things we don't need in heaven that we do need on earth. For example, we won't need our bills paid or our bodies and minds healed in heaven, but we do need those things on earth.

We, therefore, need to win some things in this earthly realm that are akin to blessings, and the blessings that we want are the blessings that come out of the gospel. We don't just want stuff for the sake of stuff. We want what the Bible has promised us. We want what God has for us based on the gospel.

In order to win, we need to have focus, and there are three things we need to focus on:

1. Focus on being better than the opponent or obstacle.

2. Focus on winning rather than losing.

3. Focus on What's Important Now (WIN).

Focusing on these key aspects of winning enables us to have a lifestyle of worship that brings victory to our lives.

BE BETTER

First, we have to focus on being better than the opponent or the obstacle. You can't be better than your opponent, who is Satan, if you're giving him all your attention. You will not win in a conflict when you're giving all your focus to the opponent or the obstacle. Instead of telling God how big your problem is, you need to start telling your problem how big your God is.

Rather than focusing on the opponent or the obstacle, we need to focus on the God in us, who enables us to be better than the opponent or the obstacle. If it weren't possible for us to be better than our opponent and our obstacles, I believe that Jesus would have taken us with Him when He ascended to heaven. He left us here so that we could do the original job of mankind, which was to have dominion over all the earth (Genesis 1:26–28). We have power and authority in this earthly realm, and we need to use it against our opponent and our obstacles.

To be better than the opponent and the obstacles, you can't wait until you're facing them in conflict. You have to start right now and better yourself before they even show up. A boxer doesn't wait until he steps into the ring to prepare for the match. He begins training long before that match is even on the horizon.

We tend to get thrown off because we don't realize what's going on until we encounter the opponent or the obstacle. But if we're living with heaven as our goal, we know that we're going to be attacked. Don't wait until the attack comes. Start preparing for it now.

David said in Psalm 144:1, "Blessed be the LORD, my rock, who trains my hands for war, and my fingers for battle." His training to fight began long before he set foot on the battlefield. Before David battled Goliath, he killed lions and bears that were threatening his father's sheep (1 Samuel 17:34–37). Don't despise God's training, because He is training you for reigning. He is getting you ready for what you're going to face. Once you get into the battle, you'll find yourself thanking Him for that training and preparation.

BE POSITIVE

Second, we need to focus on winning instead of losing. Oftentimes, the obstacle looks so huge and the opponent so big that you focus on them and start to believe that there's no way you could win. When Moses sent the twelve spies to scout out the promised land, only two of them brought back a positive report. The others said, "We came to the land to which you sent us. It flows with milk and honey, and this is its fruit. However, the people who dwell in the land are strong, and the cities are fortified and very large" (Numbers 13:27–28).

Focus on the positive, not the negative. Having to face a strong enemy was a negative, but the fact that it was a land flowing with milk and honey was a positive, as was the fact that God had promised this land to them. You need to focus on what God has said instead of what you see with your eyes. It's not always easy to stop focusing on the negative, but if you've been with God long enough, you've seen Him come through for you. Remembering what He has done for you in the past will help you to focus on the positive.

The Swedish newspaper editor and poet Carl Boberg understood well the importance of focusing on the positive as a believer. One day in the late 1800s, he was caught in a violent storm on the way home:

Lightning flashed. Thunderclaps shook the air, sending Boberg running for shelter.

When the storm began to relent, he rushed home. He opened his windows to let in the fresh bay air, and the vision of tranquility that greeted him stirred something deep in his soul. The sky had cleared. Thrushes sang, and in the distance, the resonant knell of church bells sounded. With the juxtaposition between the roaring thunderstorm and such bucolic calm as background, Boberg sat down and wrote "O Store Gud"—the poem that, through a winding series of events would become "How Great Thou Art."[19]

Sometimes life's storms, like literal storms, catch us by surprise, and it's not a pleasant experience. But instead of focusing on how he'd been soaked in the storm, Carl Boberg focused on serving the God who holds all of the natural world in His hands. Out of this understanding and the awe and reverence it inspired in him, Boberg wrote what would become one of the most beloved Christian hymns. This was possible only because, out of his faith in God, he chose to look at the positive.

When there's nothing positive around you that you can see, focus on the Lord. Habakkuk 3:17–18 says, "Though the fig tree should not blossom, nor fruit be on the vines, the produce of the olive fail and the fields yield no food, the flock be cut off from the fold and there be no herd in the stalls, yet I will rejoice in the LORD; I will take joy in the God of my salvation."

You may currently be sick, broke, depressed, or anxious, but you still have cause to rejoice in the Lord, because He has saved you by His divine power. If you have nothing else to praise God for, you can praise Him for your salvation. You can praise Him for dying on the cross for your sins and rising from the dead so that you could have new life. You can thank Him that, because of His sacrifice, you get to spend eternity in heaven with Him.

BE IN THE MOMENT

Lastly, we need to focus on What's Important Now, or WIN for short. Some of us are focused on what we missed or lost yesterday, and we need to think about what's important now. In our cars, the rearview mirror is much smaller than our windshield for a reason: our cars spend more time going forward than backward. Likewise, when it comes to our spiritual lives, we need to look forward more than we look backward. It's not about what God did yesterday, but about what He is doing now.

The hymn Boberg penned doesn't translate "How Great Thou *Were*," but rather "How Great Thou *Art*"—present tense, not past. The past matters, but our present and future are not limited to what has already transpired. After all, a team that's been losing for the entire game can still rally in the fourth quarter and come from behind to win if they're focused on the points that they will score rather than the points that have already been scored against them. We need to remember that the past doesn't constrain God.

The things that happened yesterday are lessons for tomorrow's blessings. We must learn how to live in the moment, because living in the moment brings about winning. Instead of focusing on the end goal, we need to appreciate what God is giving us right now. Otherwise, we'll miss the blessings He has for us in the present. There are powerful things happening in this moment!

After David sinned by committing adultery with Bathsheba and then having her husband, Uriah, killed, God allowed the baby Bathsheba bore to David to fall ill. David fasted and prayed while the baby was sick, but the baby died. When David was informed of the death of his child, he did something remarkable: "Then David arose from the earth and washed and anointed himself and changed his clothes. And he went into the house of the LORD and worshiped. He then went to his own house. And when he asked, they set food before him, and he ate" (2 Samuel 12:20).

People were shocked by his behavior, and David explained to them, "While the child was still alive, I fasted and wept, for I said, 'Who knows whether the LORD will be gracious to me, that the child may live?' But now he is dead. Why should I fast? Can I bring him back again? I shall go to him, but he will not return to me" (2 Samuel 12:22–23).

They had assumed that David was functioning out of desperation, but he wasn't. He was focused on what was important now. When the baby was still alive, it was important to fast and pray in the event that God might spare the baby's life. Now that the baby had died, it was important to praise and worship God. David knew that the God he served would get him through this tragedy. He had lost his son, but he was still winning in God. Winning in God is confusing to those who don't know God like we do.

Second Samuel 12:24 continues, "Then David comforted his wife, Bathsheba, and went in to her and lay with her, and she bore a son, and he called his name Solomon. And the LORD loved him." On the other side of this tragedy, of the baby who died, was the greatest, wisest, and wealthiest person who ever lived. If David had gotten mad at God and become stuck in the fact that the baby had died, it's possible that Solomon would never have been born. But David realized that what was important now was moving forward and worshiping the Lord, and God used that to bless all of Israel with Solomon's wisdom and rule.

When we focus on being better than the opponent or the obstacle, on winning instead of losing, and on what's important now, we will be victorious in the Lord. We will offer Him victorious worship that honors Him in all seasons and all situations, worship that is truly worthy, wired, wise, and winning.

Conclusion Questions

Question: Look at the list of the three things you need to focus on to win in life: focus on being better than the opponent or obstacle, focus on winning rather than losing, and focus on What's Important Now (WIN). Are you struggling to focus in these ways? What changes can you make to redirect your focus in these three key areas?

_____

_____

_____

_____

_____

_____

_____

_____

_____

_____

_____

_____

Question: What problem is vying for your attention right now? How can you redirect your focus from how big that problem is to how great your God is?

_____

_____

_____

_____

_____

_____

_____

_____

_____

_____

Question: Are there any details of your past that are keeping you from fully living in victory in the present moment? What can you do to release those experiences to the Lord and allow Him to empower you to live in the moment?

_____

_____

_____

_____

_____

_____

_____

_____

_____

_____

_____

Question: Do you take an active role of opposition toward the devil, or are you more prone to being his victim? What does God's Word say about the authority you have over the devil?

_____

_____

_____

_____

_____

_____

_____

_____

_____

_____

Action: On a sheet of paper, create two columns. At the top of one column, write, "What I See." At the top of the other column, write, "What God Has Said." How does focusing on what God has said change your perspective on your circumstances?

Conclusion Notes

_____

_____

_____

_____

_____

_____

_____

_____

_____

_____

_____

_____

_____

_____

_____

_____

About the Author

Pastor Andre Mitchell is a devoted husband and father who recognized the call of God upon his life at an early age. He is a gifted speaker with a passion for communicating God's Word through both writings and oral presentations. He preached his first sermon in November of 1997. In 2000, he married his childhood friend, Devon, and they eventually had three children together. He became a youth pastor at the age of 25 and served in that capacity until his thirty-fifth birthday, when he became the senior pastor of Deliverance Temple in Muncie, Indiana.

As pastor of DT and CEO of Andre Mitchell Ministries, he

has accumulated numerous achievements, but he cherishes the title of child of God above them all. He is known to his family as being loving, caring, responsible, and kind. He is known by his congregation as a servant leader, a prayer warrior, a relevant teacher, and a fireball preacher. He is known in his community as an author, an activist, an innovator, and a voice for the underprivileged. His personal life mission is to remain authentic in his pursuit of, passion for, and portrayal of God.

About Renown Publishing

Renown Publishing was founded with one mission in mind: to make your great idea famous.

At Renown Publishing, we don't just publish. We work hard to pair strategy with innovative marketing techniques so that your book launch is the start of something bigger.

Learn more at RenownPublishing.com.

Notes

1. Lexico, "worship." https://www.lexico.com/en/definition/worship?locale=en.

2. Lexico, "worthy." https://www.lexico.com/en/definition/worthy.

3. Lexico, "worthy."

4. Merriam-Webster, "worship." https://www.merriam-webster.com/dictionary/worship.

5. Merriam-Webster, "worship."

6. Merriam-Webster, "worship."

7. Cleveland, James, and the New Jerusalem Baptist Church Choir. "I Don't Feel Noways Tired." Track B1 on *Everything Will Be Alright.* Savoy Records, 1978, vinyl.

8. Blue Letter Bible, "Strong's H7200 – *rā'â*." https://www.blueletterbible.org/lexicon/h7200/kjv/wlc/0-1/.

9. BibleRef. "What Does Genesis 3:16 Mean?" https://www.bibleref.

com/Genesis/3/Genesis-3-16.html.

10. BibleRef, "What Does Genesis 3:16 Mean?"

11. Alsup, Wendy. "Her Desire Will Be for Her Husband." April 11, 2010. Practical Theology for Women. https://theologyforwomen. org/2010/04/her-desire-will-be-for-her-husband.html.

12. Merriam-Webster, "rich." https://www.merriam-webster.com/ dictionary/rich.

13. Francis Asbury Society, "The Good Kings of Judah: Learning to Avert Moral Failure from Eight Good Men Who Didn't." https://www.francisasburysociety.com/wp-content/uploads/Good-Kings-of-Judah-Answer-Guide_fas.pdf.

14. UCG Bible Commentary, "Introduction to Isaiah (Isaiah 1) March 12." United Church of God. https://bible.ucg.org/bible-commentary/ Isaiah/Sins-of-Israel-and-Judah-like-scarlet/.

15. Malick, David. "An Introduction to Isaiah." June 14, 2004. https:// bible.org/article/introduction-isaiah.

16. Stewart, Don. "Who Were the Samaritans?" Blue Letter Bible. https://www.blueletterbible.org/faq/don_stewart/don_stewart_1319. cfm.

17. Time. "The Bible: Superior Samaritans." April 1, 1966. Time.com. http://content.time.com/time/subscriber/article/0,33009,840623,00. html.

18. Lexico, "win." https://www.lexico.com/en/definition/win?locale =en.

19. Little, Jon. "Behind the Song: Carl Boberg, 'How Great Thou Art.'" American Songwriter. 2021. https://americansongwriter.com/behind-the-song-carl-boberg-how-great-thou-art/.